bahamian children cry

bahamian children cry

VALERIE H KNOWLES PH.D.

ISBN-13: 9781977850003
ISBN-10: 1977850006

Table of Contents

Introduction

Stabbed to Death (witnessing mother's death**)**
She touched me that morning
before starting her busy day.
Packed drinks in my lunch bag.
Clothes for P.E ironed, put away.
Last brush and grease on my hair,
I could hear her constant prayer
for Daddy to stay clear of us today.
Daddy walked drunk in the yard,
looked at her mean and hard and gave
her one more chance to take him
back with his beatin- cheatin intact.
"No, my friend, on God I'll depend,
my chirren he'll defend, for sure.
Not going back, I had enough of that!"

KNIFE flashed in the air, stabbing
without care, fear or hurry, cutting
without worry of law, Lord, or man.
She grabbed me with tears and bloody
hands, layin, prayin sayin 'love you,
forgive my friend, no revenge, let it end."
LIFE left we and never came back again

bahamian children cry saying; *'Some of us are weary, stumbling, and falling. Infuse us with power so that we may mount up with wings like eagles, so that we may run and remain steady; so that we may walk and not faint (Isaiah 40:29-31 adapted).*

When we interact with talented, competent Bahamian children (of which there are many), a sense of pride easily envelopes us. In the same way, feelings of powerlessness can envelope us when we encounter children who are stifled and weighed down with adult-like burdens. These burdens could have come from (a) the many facets of negative social change (b) irresponsible parenting or (c) from the children's own poor decision- making skills. The 2014 IDB Citizens Security and Justice Report in reviewing data from the Royal Bahamas Police Force, noted that the homicide rate in the Bahamas more than doubled in the last decade. In 2013, 37% of homicide victims were males under age 25. Armed robberies increased 81% (from 199 in 2004 to 361 in 2013). Reported rapes increased by 17% since 2004. In addition to this, there are innumerable children experiencing loss of family members as a result of death from cancers, and deaths from other non-communicable diseases (diabetes, lupus, hypertension etc.). While some children may be affected by any one of the mentioned variables, there are many cases where children simultaneously wrestle with all the above.

We know that our children are challenged in many ways. Yet we want them to resolve their challenges even as they attain the expected milestones of healthy child and adolescent development. What are the healthy, positive behavioral benchmarks that we should be helping our children to attain?

Healthy Ego Development vs Egocentrism, Narcissism
We expect to see strong, healthy egos emerging from the turbulence of our children's childhood and adolescent life experiences. There is the expectation that children will struggle to attain better control of their impulses. They should struggle to establish stronger intellectual control over their emotions as they learn to restrain themselves under duress. The society expects that our young ones would learn to wait. This would

be noticed in their enhanced capacity to tolerate the frustration and tension that comes with waiting. This involves learning to put aside something immediately pleasurable but short-lived while waiting to accomplish something of more lasting importance.

Healthy Social Relationships

When our adolescents are forming healthy social relationships, we expect them to develop a stronger capacity to accept the strength and weakness of others. We hope to see them developing the ability to mourn relationship losses while learning to establish new connections that are empathetic, reciprocal, meaningful, and hopefully stable. We look for an emerging sense of competence. This sense of competence should be growing as adolescents learn to manage themselves and respond to the demands placed on them by their families and the larger society.

Holistic Cognitive, Affective, Language Development

Reasoning, memory and language skills should become stronger. Healthy adolescents are usually individualistic yet peer-focused, idealistic yet creative. They should be omnipotent dreamers with the capacity to intellectually and emotionally relax by delving into music, art, dance, theatre. Healthy adolescents should sleep well. We expect them to be open to new experiences while maintaining clear boundaries between themselves and others.

REMEMBER

Many times, the impact of an experienced trauma negatively influences the journey to health. However, the impact of the trauma is not always noted right away. The full impact may only surface when children act out their distress. Sometimes they go for years with the pain bottled up inside. Some grow up, live and die without ever facing up to the pain caused by their experiences. It is good to note that despite their trauma, Bahamian children, like other children can be resilient. Time and time again, stories of overcomers and 'never-give-uppers' light up the horizon to motivate all concerned. With this in mind, we should resolve to treat all children with special care. We may not know what is happening in their lives. Whether they are in group homes, foster care, legal incarceration, on the street, in the food stores, at school, let these stories motivate you to reach out and interact with young people in a manner that helps the nurturing and healing processes.

Understanding the Book
Framework for Analysis

bahamian children cry is <u>not</u> a poetry book. The writings were not meant to conform to any literary style or literary rules. Snapshots of stressful events in the life of selected Bahamian children are presented. Complex stories are reformatted to highlight the main thoughts and feelings of the child during the experience. As you read each epigraph, consider some of the questions outlined below. These questions will help you reflect on how each situation can impact the development of the child involved.

1. **IMPACT ON IDENTITY**: How does the experience affect the child's image of him/herself? Is this a positive or negative image? How does this image affect the child's learning and behavior? As a result of this experience, how do you think this child answers questions such as, "Who am I? Who am I like? Who do I want to be like?"

2. **IMPACT ON SENSE OF PURPOSE**: How do you think the child in this experience answers questions such as, "What am I here for? What am I supposed to be doing with my life now?" How does this sense of purpose affect the child's learning and behavior?

3. **SENSE OF COMPETENCE**: What behaviors are being rewarded in this experience? What skills are being developed? Is it a constructive skill base or a destructive skill base that is being developed? How does this sense of competence affect the child's learning and behavior?

4. **SENSE OF BELONGING:** How do you think the child answers questions such as, "To whom am I special? Who cares about me? Who do I care about? Is there a special attachment to a parent or

some other person? How does this attachment affect the child's learning and behavior?

5. **SENSE OF SECURITY**: In the experience, 'Who accepts the child regardless of faults?' Consider, how does the child answer questions like these, "Who is with me even when I am at my lowest point?" Is this supportive person a parent or some other person? How does this rooting of the child's sense of security affect the child's learning and behavior?"

6. **PLACE IN THE WORLD**: Based on the way persons are interacting with the child how do you think the child would answer these questions: 'Whose laws should rule my life? "To whom am I most accountable, God, the law, my parents, myself or other?"

Part One: Models of Masculinity

"Where are the men?" This question can be easily answered, "Right where we placed them!" It seems that some elements in our society cultivate thuggery. The way we construct our masculine identities leaves little room for intelligentsia, sensitivity, artistic creativity, monogamy and fidelity in the preferred male identity. If a young man does not demonstrate any semblance of roughness or coarseness, he risks being classified as effeminate. With this classification comes stigmatization and alienation.

An intelligent, childless, academically competent, sensitive man, over the age of thirty, who is not known to be practicing serial polygamy is not likely to be taken seriously by a large segment of the society. His profile is likely to strike distrust in the hearts of many. Many of the distrusting would include some of those complaining that good men are hard to find. How many males are going to be motivated to pursue character development and academic excellence in such a hostile milieu? How many will be encouraged to remain financially embarrassed for years while they pursue higher education? It is important to give attention to the cultural messages being sent to our young men.

The voices below are the voices of young people caught in the throes of developing manhood, trying to respond to the many different models and messages of masculinity.

Be a Man Boy
(Models of Violence)

Burst da nigga, boy, show him you ain't no punk!
Chap him boy, stab him, and burst him in he mouth.
Dat nigga dissin your ma boy, dese niggas take you for light.
Doon let niggas punk you boy, pick up dat knife and fight.

Gata get respect boy, doon let niggas take ya stripe!
You need to force down da girl boy, hurry break her in.
She braggin here bout she a virgin, force the ting ma boy.
You need to get it right, you mussy like man hey, Mr. Polite.

If she say "no" boy, she dissin you, callin ya light, break in
your girlfriend boy, I is ya Pa. I learnin you about ya rights!
Break down da jail cell boy, rape charge can't keep you in.
Bribe someone boy, find one a ya street brethren!

Burst one a dem prisoner' boy, so dey could see you een light.
Don't bend over for no break-in boy, know ya prisoner's rights
Chap the walls away boy, chapter quietly every night.
Burst dem mental chains boy, for generations, holdin' you tight.

Udder Niggaz Gun

(gang war over girls)

Udder Niggaz grip my shirt man,
slam me hard tween my eye.
I whap him wid my cutlass,
I burst 2 bottle in he eye.
Dey throw more rock on me,
one ketch me on my chin.
My boys run dem down and
cave dey bloody head in,
Four dey boys try rush us,
thought they slick for sure;
I swing round da big knife
and slice up four more;
Don't' think this finish yet.
Yo, must deal with my gun!
You want live, Udder Niggaz,
you'll better start ya run.

Down the road *was* walking
now runnin, runnin for my life.
Knife, can't help me nah.
Is all-out dawg to death fight.
Gunshots lickin, hittin, stickin
as Udda Niggaz drive by fast.
I hear the siren loud, screamin,
blood pumpin, I bleedin fast.
Darkness here everywhere,
and none of my boys in sight.
Face down, in the loneliness,
Jah know erryting is aight.

I glad my gal was watchin,
watchin how suicidal I fight.
For sure she *now* know I een
like Udder Niggaz, I een light.
Before she talk to dem Niggaz
again, I know she ga tink twice.
See she at my wake now, nice.
T-shirt, pum-pum shorts, white
Drink and pain, the funeral rites.
Scripture, solos, eulogy, aight!
How come nobody braggin
bout how good I could a fight?
Mamma won't stop screaming.
Sisters and brothers, ill on the floor.
"Heh, big up my fightin more!
My gal need to tell you'll the tale.
I bad, I beat plenty Udder Niggaz
I put plenty a dem, young in jail!
Get my legacy right, I wasn't light!
Just talkin to my gal, made this a
death fight!"

Crazy Nigga
(mother's new boyfriend)

Dis Nigga playin bae.
He better stop.
Dis house jam up
and dis hard floor hot!
How long, he ga be here,
holdin up my room?
Doon live here, and
he een wan go home!
You een my daddy, son!
In here, lazy leg cross!
Can't touch me, cappy.
In here I is da boss!
Twice a day, 7 on da hour,
dis stupid Nigga in here,
hoggin up our shower.
Bold; but *I* gat power!
In da kitchen there,
openin pot on stove.
Dis Nigga wan us get up,
and iron *he* clothes!
Playin in he hair, see
my ma freakin on he knee,
Wan *my* sisters get up
to make dis crazy Nigga
corn beef, grits and tea!
"Shet ***** up",
he like to holler,
searchin my ma bag
for condoms and dollar.

Callin he gals dem, loud
my ma cell in he hand.
Dis lazy Nigga say he ga
teach *me* to be man!!!
He steppin cold over my
brudders dem who sleepin
on hard floor, dis Nigga
disrespectin, he doin for more!
I will work this out, change
this plan, *I* ga teach this Nigga
this bold Nigga to be a man!
In the house, his plate full a meat.
I slap him hard, breaking teeth.
He een no daddy over we!
My foot on him, he can't go far
Comin here in udder gal car!
"You, leave him lone" mudda say
"I gats needs and bills to pay.
Don't need you getting in my way
Find ya sef some place to stay."

Thug for Life
(reward for crime)

People crying about my juvenile delinquency.
Me, 14 and dey wan know what I ga be!
And they don't make more money than me!
Even my family does borrow money ya see!

Dey always warning me about jail time.
It's part of the risk, I don't pay it much mind.
I watch them slaving, no rest, 10-hrs a day.
Yet old house, old car, and retiring with small pay.

Handcuffed, beaten, known on the streets,
police lock me up four times already, at least.
Each time, skills and fearlessness, they increase!
More clothes, girls, bling, more life of treats!

Each lock up, big up my name and my street score,
Gals, soldiers, thug/man respect me even more.
That soft boy life too girly, it ain't really for me,
Rewards, too far ahead, impossible to clearly see.

Kind people of hypocrisy, amorality, duplicity,
courageously accusing young people just like me.
I don't care if I get lock up and beat up again,
Anywhere they put me, I'll meet some friends.

My Mudda Girlfriend
(mother's lesbianism)

Mudda girlfriend was waiting for me outside the shop, if she tink I scared a she, she better stop, she say out loud she hard, but me, I born tough, wan take over my family, she wan play rough.

I look round to see if anyone did hear, dis big teet red woman, with her beer, orange hair, trying to cause me fear, I look round, pick up one rock, I fling it and it just miss her and the shop.

"Boy, I don't understand your problem with me and ya ma, I takin care a you'll better dan ya'll no good pa, respect da love between me and ya ma, dis hate for me and her gone too far.

And don't be fool, takin family business to school, if dey question our love, we ga say no, that you is the problem, you uncontrollable, make up ya mind, respect our love or all-out war with me.

You better get use to it boy, we is a couple, we done out, I tired a your trouble, when I come round dat house, sweet boy, I gat clout, get with the program or you could get the ***out.

Out, to plenty girls I went, mating to get rid of feared genetic-gay stench, to other homes we went, living all over the place until police find us and brought us back again to our mudda face.

My mudda leave dat girlfriend, she got a younger man, I try to stay home, away from step daddy friendly hand, I fightin, holding the tide, knowing mudda and her girlfriend sneakin on the side.

Destructive Anger

(beating to scar)

WHAP! WHAP! WHAP!
"When I called you,
        WHAP!
why you didn't come?
        WHAP!
You know I don't
********play around!
"I'll kick your ******
black ****** all over
this**** ground."

Good solid whaps
across my face slap.
Swinging at my back
new marks linkin up
with belt scars sitting
already on the tract.

"I tell you before
don't ****with me
You is one big,
black, stupid, boy
good for nuttin, see,
wuttless and dumb
where you come from?
When I call you again
you wutless, ogly boy
you better run and come.

You een learnin****
in school,****
get your dumb****
out and go work if
you don't want get hurt

Never Be the Same
(tired but trapped)

I sick and tired of waking up every morning hearing about a fight, hearing about hurting somebody, hearing someone bragging about how they hurt somebody, hearing fellas dem planning to hurt somebody. Everybody talking about the struggle being real, about making that paper (money). Hurt or be hurt, everybody all the time talking about disrespect.

Everything is a disrespect, it's like some fellas ain' happy unless they can find a disrespect, because now they have a chance to wibe, to fight, to get attention, to show their strength. Some bredrin 'get off' on hurting people. Some dudes ain't really into this, but they do not know how to get out.

Yes, I hang around with the 'fellas' but in my mind, I never do nuttin serious. I would never start a fight or hit somebody but if they were holding a gun on somebody, I would be the one to take they phone or search they pocket for the money, take off the watch etc.

I would look out to see if anybody was coming, would be one of those running in the opposite direction from where the main fellas was running if there was a chase. Nobody could out run me. While the fellas was running, sometimes I would be the one to hide the stuff until we got back together.

Yes, I have seen someone killed before, more than once, I have listened to plans to murder, heard it get contracted out, been with fellas when they ordered a 'body bag' and had people try give me a contract for a 'body bag', but everybody know that wasn't my thing.

Like I said, my friends would beat someone about the body
or in their head with wood and ting, or use brass knuckles to harm,
injure other people. I never set out to kill anybody. Beat them bad, yes
but not to kill them. I would watch, or surround the fella, making up the
numbers to intimidate the person so they be scared when they fighting.

The worst experiences for me was being in a group where
they 'jick up a nigga' (stabbing a victim multiple times) and blood got
on me, one time we were robbing one man and he keep trying to
fight and trying to get away and they kick him down and stomp him
and throw rock on his head when he fell down and I searched while he
was unconscious to see if he had any money on him. The fellas dem
had to knock him out, so he wouldn't get up and try call the police
before we got away.

I am not going to do this forever. I plan on getting a job but my G.P.A
ain't too good and people think I gang bang because I run with those
fellas but that is not true. I don't consider myself a banger but all this talk
about leaving, I have to put on hold cuz these bredrin tell me until they
could trust me out of the group, I have to put my leaving plans on hold.

Part Two: Personal Struggles

Bahamian children are troubled with the same issues that negatively affect children in other nations. Just over a decade ago, a 2005 IDB report, *The Situation of Youth in the Bahamas*, indicated that certain Bahamian youth were affected by crime, violence, unstable home environments, poor academic histories, poor labour market realities, poverty, learning disabilities, mental health challenges, and poor sexual and reproductive health situations. Bahamian children were worried too about having a successful schooling experience. They were also concerned about whether they would be able to find employment upon graduation.

Some children worried about violence, whether they would become victims of violence. There were fears about becoming pregnant or making someone else pregnant. A 2008 National Institute of Health report indicated that about 30% of Bahamian students under the age of 16 were sexually experienced at the time of the survey. About 57% of students over the age of 16 were found to be sexually involved. There were students who had a fear of contracting HIV and or a fear of being sexually abused.

The UNAIDS report for 2013 noted that there were 7,816 persons believed to be living with HIV in the Bahamas. This means that since 2013 there were at least 7,816 impacted children in this category. If some of the affected persons were part of a family that included more than one child, this significantly increased the number of impacted children. To draw a clearer picture of the extent of childhood stressors, we need to add to these tragedies the number of children impacted by an estimated 500 homicides within the last five years.

The voices below echo the conflict of youth responding to the obstacles thrown into their lives. Some of the voices below reflect struggles with learning disability and mental health issues among other complex issues.

Mudda Sick
(student father)

My gal 13 and pregnant, mudda sick NOW!
Dey tell me use condom but didn't say HOW!
Don't need to worry, from dis I ga walk.
I too young for dem to take me to court.

I should play fool, say baby ain't mine,
I only been dere dat one time, mudda sick Boo
What I suppose to do, my head screw!
I too young and dis ain't right, but I ain't
ga let her pregnancy jam up my life.

My ole lady wan know what I tellin her for,
she ain't gat nuff for us, much less one more,
don't wan nobody parents crowdin her door,
I hate to see her pregnant, sad, out of school,
I like her, it ain't fair, this here ain't cool!

She wan me come over to visit and talk,
I hail, chat fast, and speed walk, I gat exam.
For a girl her age, she gat hot homicidal rage.
Mudda sick, no money, no clue and baby due.
We cook dis pot but can't eat the stew.

I bring my Saturday $50 tip and tip in awe.
Glad for the time to play with son on the floor.
She yuck him from my hand, for her new man,
take my fifty dollars and run me off dey land.

Passin the gate, anger heavy in my hand,
my son and my girl playin with another man,
Mudda sick dread I can't pay, so can't play,
ain't gat nuttin I could do but walk away.

What kind a life could baby mama give my son?
Stress, hate for me, step-daddy drama and confusion
Must hurry forward in school, take advantage
of that single parent, 'no-affidavit-no daddy' rule.

My Bird Neck
(emotional violence)

In my yard behind the stoop,
I kept my pigeon in a handmade coop.
Saved lunch money to buy bird seed,
I was really proud of my good deed.

Sometimes it ate out of its own bird pan.
Sometimes it ate from the palm of my hand.
Sometimes, it flew from far away tree,
came right home to land beside me.

I'd let it out to get a flap, fly far away
but it always, somehow found its way back.
Loved my pigeon, wanted to call it Roy,
could never be sure if was girl or boy.

One day it came back with a friend,
I thought my joy would never end!
"Listen hard head boy, you can't hear?"
Too much bird dem comin round here!

Turn da bird loose, it makin a mess,
and all dem droppins causin me stress.
Stop wastin my money buyin bird seed,
Use my money to buy something you need!"

One day my bird did mess on the porch,
mudda look mad, she was distraught.
I protected my bird close to my chest,
Mudda yuck it from me and pop he neck!

My Daddy's Name
(drug dealer's son)

My mummy gave me my daddy's name,
To share his glory not his shame.
But man, my life has been a living hell,
the pressure and pain, I know so well
bearing the shame of a drug dealing name.

So tired being tied to the face on the screen
Of the name of captured murder suspect #3,
'#3 captured on the run', reporter begun
volume low, only the picture show
of cuffed, natty dread my daddy, suspect #3

Close up of victim's bloody shirt for all to see,
Reporter of poor taste, smiling at camera, and me.
Rude microphone thrust in mourning son face,
up the distressed nostrils of family of victim of #3.
This hysterical reporter of no simple sensitivity

Dad, convicted, dread locks cut from his head
tumble on my not-ready shoulders instead.
On the park, evading vigilante, fear, clear, dark.
Time to cut hair and leave here and flee fear.
But no place to erase image of daddy's victim #3

I take flight in weed to escape my father's deed.
Me in weed escaped on the park, when cold fellas
came throwing message at me to find the Kilo
my father steal, that Kilo would set ole man free,
while erasing legal fee and mortal debt left to me

In the night, on the court, daddy's mantle heavy on me,
Took a shot, missed, pressure, strain, mental pain.
Cold fellas grabbed rebound, tired playin round.
"Where your ole man hide the Kil, find it, sell it or
bring it to we, our Kil, your key, fee to be free.

Say they could see my ole man hidden in me,
"Your daddy, the prison heir, full of confidence,
has no fear, that you could find his Kil, the key
to buy a lawyer and again set him and you free."
Come to the prison, he wanted to talk to me.
But through the prison bars I could only see
freedom from name- chains urgently calling me.
Convicted, his life sentence, did set me free.
No desire to appeal him free, to mis-identify me.
Should I sell the Kil for he, or for me and safety?

I left the neighborhood with the Kil, his appeal,
buried, safe without trail to me of new hair, no fear,
for years new name, no shame until they found me
paid by cold fellas to beat me to get the payment Kil.
Beaten, broken, they left me, unconscious but not dead

'Don't kill him, boy I scared, you know who son this is,
dread, I een wan dead', leave him, and we lie instead.
Say, at secret spot, he headshot, dismembered and dead.
Peaceful, happy, pain, smothered my betrayal shame.
Daddy Name, my life spared because of my daddy's name.

Soft Boy
(male exploitation)

Dese slick gals round here
don't wan be seen wid me,
Say I is a nerd, a *SOFT BOY*
I don't have no fresh SUV.
My plain, homely *SOFT BOY*
clean shirt ain't enough ya see,
Say I must wear Sean-Johns,
Hill-Figgers, or fresh Tommy!

Geemee dollar, geemee, geemee
snack, geemee, geemee phone card,
geemee dis ting, and geemee dat!
Don't they get it, dey mussy trippin;
and me and dem in same class sittin
in <u>same</u> student position, yet me,
I, must hurry find money to pay,
SOFT BOY extortion fee, everyday

So instead a studyin, I start to work.
Packin people grocery till it hurt.
So, when geemee gals come beg me,
I free from their public blast and shame
of having to be called 'Broke Nigga'
adding public shame to my name, yo
I turn into a real geemee gals' man.
Sure to have extra money in hand

Then G.P.A gone down below 3.3!
Bae dis extortion stoppin now ya see!

When next these geemee gals beg,
I callin out my name, 'SOFT BOY'
I ain't scared! I saying this for me
"Dis soft boy here, boss, he gone free.
You'll, stop mistakin me fa ya missin
trifflin, dead-beat, cold daddy!"

Don't sleep geemee gals organize, ya'll!
Ready to beg and, shame, always on call.
Without work, makin 100 dollars a night,
From money from fellas scared a the call.
Gals without gall who ga call dem light.
Fellas too afraid, scared to shout out 'no,'
Extortin geemee gals gat dem all in tow!

Dey den turn round and complain,
how black man, dey always broke.
But we lock up in ya geemee choke.
This soft boy makin a huge change,
I stop this game takin a stand, givin
you my money won't make me a man,
Steppin out dis greedy geemee plan,
And hey I still is the realest man!

I too smart to play this slick game plan!
Call me soft, blast me, I ain't shame!
I learn a 'Soft Boy' is a sensible man.
He usin he head to think, progress and plan.
Call me soft, call me hater, guess what
I ga have all hard earned my money now.
And I will have even more money later!

I Don't Care
(parental drug abuse and HIV)

I am reckless and violent, cold
heartless, obscene and profane.
Stealing, cursin, fightn, partyin
It's still my call, rules, my game.
My weak conscience I defend.
I sold rapes of 3 my good friends
for fun and game and pimp money.
No fear, you'll know I don't care!
When it was my hurtin abuse time,
no one helped me cope or escape.
No one cared about my life, my fate.
Don't talk to me, you'll can't do nuttin
more to hurt, punish or control me!

Mum was fine, saw her decline
From fun to discrimination misery.
Before she died, she with no pride
in the nasty job she gave to me.
Watch the door, move condoms
from the floor, tell customers
to have a seat" if want to eat.
A job I did well, under the spell
of her selling and full-blown HIV.

You'll don't stress and trouble me.
This drug dealer really care bout me!
He say I young, I can still have fun,
even if he is a criminal on the run.
I did hide his drugs, hide he gun,

drive a stolen car all, just for fun
Because he cares, he gets to share
our things, with my friends and me,
Young, free is how thug life is be.
And right now, I really don't care.
Get out my face, it's too, too late.
I really don't have to care, I mean
I really am too scared to think or care.

Must Scream
(autism-learning disability)

Eyes wide, bold, yet not seeing.
All the faces the same to me.
I am so very unique, different.
I really Scream in pain if it rains
and even if you touch me softly
tenderly, I still shriek and Scream.

Even clothes make me scream,
I can't stand the feel of any cloth
passing over my sensitive skin.
Only lining up my things seems
to ease the real misery felt within.

I line things up all through the night.
I line them up all through the day.
When I line things up, no touching
is so they must stay as I sing and play.
A straight line, I'll have it no other way.

I Scream in the car going to school,
because the red light wouldn't move
and my world crumbles, I become angry,
I am not amused, I do holler and scream.
My poor parents are baffled, so confused!

I love to draw, but I can't even write.
I will swallow, but won't try to bite.
I sing long songs well but cannot talk,

Never crawled, just jumped up, walked.
Only learned to smile after age three.

Toilet training was and still not for me
Many days across our polished floor,
dragged, pulled screaming with tantrums
through the open unwelcome bathroom door.
Toilet bowl eight years, never unused.
Only in my pants, no toilets, I refused.
Sudden, public noises with emissions
unbidden, escape me, others' noses held.
Shocked people, they must really hate me.

My confused parents are lost, can't understand
I continually grab their hands to make demands.
Laugh in space, while endlessly banging my face,
on padded walls partially covered to protect me.
It' s a mystery you see, I can dance to any song
any genre of melody but I fight, spit and Scream
if someone tries to dance my melody beside me.
My parents always ask, 'What's to become of me?'

Shame No More
(teacher insensitivity to clinical hyperactivity)

Shame looked in my face as I see others sit still and write answers so perfectly. When will my time come, I hope it be soon, I'll be turning thirteen in June, hours studying and still can't pass, can't stop talkin, always last, yet I could help others do *their* work in class!

Shame bent over, coming closer to shout in my ear, so loud the whole school hear, " Lil boy, I glad you ain't mine, cause I would a done tear up your rude behind, sit down and keep ya hip still I say, or you ain't going out for lunch again today!"

Been to lunch only once this week, keep being punished for talkin and being out of seat, try to sit, but the class dem too long, my feet won't behave, they keep taking me along, I try to write the many ideas in my head, but my fingers and mouth, playin another game instead.

Shame's hand over me stretched, grabbed my throat, stifled my breath as I looked at my page and could see, though repeating this grade twice, I was getting another D thrice, dying to be free, only real hope, in *Favorites* Junkanoo, Technical Drawing, Art and P.E.

In Junkanoo lesson my man, I be anything I can, Shame can't hold me down in the chair, knows in a little while he'll be out a here; for the next couple lessons, *I'll* be the man, Shame won't have a place to stand; mind set, ready to go, come on time, please go slow!

Period change, I find my place, first in PE in every race, first in field events then class for Art, awesome performance from untrained hands, me, a disciplined man. Practicing, every day, by myself, even in the rain, pasting, drumming and rushin, no place for Shame.

Shame follows me home, proud medals over my back, "Stop staring at them stupid medals boy, das a bunch a crap, can't put them in the bank boy, ya can't get a job with dat, how you ga make it in life boy, with only shack and track, foolishness boy, das only a trap."

"Ya can't write one good story, ya believe ya could succeed, put dem medals way boy, try learn to read, face it boy, all ya people dem dumb, dey only farmers, good for cursin and drinkin rum, don't know boy, who you tryin to fool, only wastin time and money in da school."

Can't let Shame beat me, I gat ta stick this out, I ain't givin Shame the power to put me out, I'll keep trying to focus better, concentrate the best I can, listen to what *Favorites* teach me, to improve what I can, may not get Maths trophy, no matter, I will always try to be the best I can.

White Boy Dilemma
(racial profiling stress)

Not rich but white that's alright if ya'll would only let it be,
don't go certain places, can't afford certain schools, my
parents they drive a Benz, but they ain't gat no jewels, no
swimming pools, no maid to wash our dishes, and no yard
for man to rake, no, we white, we do alright without
a house and yacht behind the exclusive beached gates,
not rich but white that's alright if the narrow- minded people
would only let it be, we white and we almost always broke,
and for some that's a joke but ya'll just need to let it be,

Now Seddy, he rich, he white and it still ain't right and the
people still criticizing him and won't let the poor boy be.
He rich and he white with all kind a knights, butlers for day
and the night, maids for his family, maid to wake him up and a
maid to put him sleep and a maid to wash they dishes with a
trained foreign maid to prepare everything their heart wishes,
a man to grow the flowers, a man to clean the car, a silent
man to chauffeur them home drunk from their weekend bars

Seddy go to a rich school and he have to work dead hard,
but nuttin he do, could fix he outrageous school report card.
Some other rich boys een white, but somehow, they smart,
dey two parents, professional Bahamians who too work hard
Now even the children of the expats they don't even get B,
I don't understand dis poor grade ting wid rich, white, Seddy.
White with tutor and money and maid ya see, nobody expected
him to come home with Cs and Ds and hardly no A with few B

He white, he rich, family prestige, for generation work hard,
building condos, owning insurance, malls, money real, no fads
They own and selling plenty land with beach and quieted title.
Look and see, 85% of money in this country for family of Seddy.
If CDs is what Seddy money buy, can't kill him, he does try.
Because CDs not for them, serious pressure they all put on him
Their money suppose to buy lawyer, financier, Ph. D not F.C.D.

Man that kind of pressure did give Seddy some serious stress.
Seddy say, 'take a rest', like them he had a plan, he ga sell land
and read any plan to construct the most complicated tall building
anywhere in town while he trap and sell crawfish, boating tourist
to the deep and dredge da sand, he tell dem open dey eye and see,
take comfort, his apple ain't fallin too far from his parents' tree.

For Seddy finding the right, white girl to date was even harder bro.
Everywhere he go, most people he know, was his family though.
Pressure for Seddy, too hard to stand, they send him to a foreign land.
Over there, he need not be a scholar, no expectation for his color
His friends for sure were not family though, real friendships, he knows
Curious folk they think you "Exotic, Sun-Tanned", coming from the sea
Very little, open interest in his family, money and political pedigree
Yep bein poor and white could be alright if the people would only let ya
be.

Being rich, white and not academically bright, could be good when
understood
How the apple was not going to fall too far from the entrepreneur family
tree

War Within

(gender diffusion difficulties)

There is a voice, insistent on my internal telephone.
Something wrong, urgent caller won't leave me alone.
Just off the basketball court, Jr. free throw champ,
top-scorer award, athletic, handsome, brainy and tall.
This is no time, to let someone peep, behind my wall.

Athletics, good defense, good cover, for this offence.
Again, my persistent internal telephone rings in my mind,
shattering my consciousness, stabbing me from behind.
My head forced under water, my lungs hurt, forcing me
to drink denial water and accept what I learned to be dirt.

This thing is stalking me inside trying to force me out.
In the gym watching, boys sweating, pulsating on the court,
the phone rings again, catching me lost in mid forbidden thought.
Pain sliced open my back, rubbing salt in the hidden crack,
I don't want anybody to know, that I prefer men though,

What kind of body have I been born with', brain chimes in?
I have hair covering all my chest, all over my face, and chin,
thick hair on my skin, but the female inside me, jumps, spins,
feeling warm, girly, really feminine, ring, that impulse, again!
Caller on the other end, wants me to go look for a boyfriend.

What kind of life will I have then, will my wrist flop or bend?
Thoughts and impulses keeps pressing me, calling me out,
I stall, don't want people scorn me, hate me, want girls date me,
Tormented, living in fear, roaring lions and phone calls in my ear,
Who will win this fierce, merciless battle raging, denied within me?

Haunted
(mental illness)

I can see one big centipede
crawling over my sheet,
Fighting with the big rat
chewing on my feet.
How come no one else
sees these things but me!
Voices command me
to cut myself.
I run to get the big
knife from off the shelf.

Terror all around, big
snakes on the ground.
On the way to school,
I flee, cars winking at me.
Men found me and
chewed pieces of my body.
All through the night,
awake in fright I stay.
no condition for stress
of school the next day

When will this 12-yr. old
child come out to eat?
Only after someone moves
that demon off her seat.
"Please come to the front
room and watch TV".
Only if pictures on the walls

stop talking to me.
See my chair move,
its rising high in the air!
Anybody else see these things,
does anybody care?
4 times tried to kill myself,
terrified by nightmares.
Parents tried everything in
foreign and doctors here.
grave dust, nor medicine worked,
I need my own prayer
to free my haunted soul
of this terrifying, ungodly fear.

Drunken Mother
(public shame)

Rum glazed my mother's eyes that stared blankly in space
in the place of rum and eager men of few dollars.
So she goes to dance four songs solo, lipstick smeared
around her mouth, but no suitors followed

Sitting outside the bar room door watching she.
Hoping she won't see me, curse me, kick me, beat me,
send me home unable to come to her rescue,
from unscrupulous, eager men of few dollars.

Must stay hidden til the right drink,
hits the right spot, and I could drag her
home before party start on the basketball court.
Mother when drunk, always wanted to wild dunk.

Mother downed much rum, fast men want fun
Like uncounted times before, I stepped to the fore.
I too, moved fast, so mummy couldn't pass
and slip away to them, from me.

Too late, party start, how will I pass
this basketball game with my drunken mother?
Other way too long, nine years old, too young,
ain't strong enough to support my drunken mother.

So I began the basketball trek.
With silent steps, on the court I go, as I tow,
my pride and her hide, swallowing glares
and stares at my drunken dunkin mother.

How long is too long before I start to drown
under the weight of my own drunken mother?

Drug Lady
(friend's violate mother)

Heard my friends brag,
bout one ole hag,
Exchanging best sex
for little money.
Hopped in the car,
they said it wasn't far.
I should see and
be with this Honey.
Dollars in my shirt,
a little fun won't hurt
and I ran in full haste
for fun car.
Underage drivers speed,
hurry to fill a need,
for some fun from
this ole Honey.
As the car turned,
the bend, the journey
came to an end as
the old hag was my
cocaine-addicted, ole lady.

Ganja Swing

(marijuana addiction)

My lazy brother offers suddenly
to weed the yard but the whole yard
he doesn't clean, just that special part
behind the old screen so he
could tend his Weed in our bushy yard.

He supposed to be pulling up the weeds
but that Weed instead was planting seed
inside his head, while rooting its leaves
and need inside him pulling up his heart.
Brother was losing the battle from the start.

When Weed calls brother comes.
Ready for school, not without weed.
Afterschool, and late evening, Weed feeds.
For something supposed to set brother free,
That plant seemed bossy and controlling to me.

Brother can't remember much, most of the time.
Weed swingin him, slow, makin him slim,
Sittin there always with that clueless grin.
Weed, young and strong, holdin it down
being sure to shut brother's reproduction down

Might as well award my brother good
Make him king, give him the prize and
the ring cause that brother he really get
swing, he think he the boss but Weed,
world boss controlling everything.

Drug Pad

(trafficking cocaine)

At the tender
age of eight,
sitting with worry
on my face
I remember
at the airport gate,
I couldn't walk straight
and before my smart
mummy had time
to fake outrage and hate
" smarter policewoman
searched my
packed privates
parts and found
cocaine packets
mummy had
put in my fake
sanitary pad".

Policeman Vex

(extortion)

Policeman vex,
He say,
we ain't gat no respect
He say,
for the immigration laws of this great country.
He say,
Give him $500 and he'll let us stay
He say,
or he calling Immigration for all a we today
He say
give him $500 or give him a name
He say,
of another illegal who could pay this game
He say,
he's the law, he vex and need money
He say,
We ain't gat no respect
He say,
say for the laws of his great country.

Dead Dog
(killing my pet)

We buried my dog today,
he came by our Hiding Box
to play in the bush
when we were hiding
from immigration 11 am
in the morning.

That Box they would never
have found if in front of it
that dog didn't whine and
run around trying to play
with me, daddy and mummy
hiding, praying inside.

My hero daddy ran outside
leaving me and mummy
inside and daddy this time
they again took away
for his usual short trip and stay.

Rat Poison in his food to eat,
I put my friend, my dog to sleep
hoping his pain, too long, didn't stay.
We needed The Box in the
bush to hide to stay, he needed
to die for play, God forgive
me for this deed today.

Dug a hole for my soul today,
by the Box where he came to play,
giving us away,
wrapping my conscience,
gray, cold stiff in sheet,
heaping on the dirt slowly,
ignoring my changing heartbeat,
in response to high price we children
pay to stay, for life every day.

Immigration Fee
(the price)

child of Haitian L'Overture snaked up Bahamian tree in the land of a
foreign brother freed by example of L'Overture's forefathers who left
him for fodder to Aristide whims and Macoute order, sitting, watching
in stealth for signs of unwilling plane tickets, watching, with envy his
sisters, for a fee, "free" to birth fruit and eat fruit to bind them to this
deceptive, promised land.

Anger mocks him who, for a fee swam carnivorous shores into indignity
to first sleep in bushes without lights in his toilet, still listening to
laughter just beyond his reach, crying for families of swimming friends
pulled from beside him by strong currents' cruel outriders that
mercilessly shatter dreams of posterity purchased with that bloody fee.

Some say they smell him stigma, strong, rank, stench, haitian oppression
and freedom still weeding, seeding, pruning yards of proud, ignorant
masters unknowingly showing him keys to vaults which Toussaint
can see, bears no fee when he constitutionally free, sets policy for
captivity in impotency, for masters unable to flee or raise fee for self or
children's ransom plea.

Ex- master of Toussaint L'Overture now staked to Bahamian tree for a
fee on the authority of his brother freed by their father for fodder to
political whims and oppression, watching his children once free, for a
fee, now weeding, seeding, bearing, selling Toussaint's fruit for sleep
and light with power just beyond his reach, hindsight and political vision.

They smell Toussaint's stigma, strong, rank, stench, Haitian oppression, and elevation, now begging him who for a fee now swim in dignity, cautious with wealth, proud notches on Toussaint's belt, holstered legitimately over strong hips, taking sisters without fee to bear fruit in sun, sand and legitimate –sea binding him tightly to his Promised Land purchased with his bloody, tears and political fee

O.G. and T.G. Dem
(Survival)

'Little Sally water, settle in da saucer, rise Sally, rise Sally,
wipe your weary eyes Sally… Singing *their* ring play songs
my lil' brother and me step into THEIR Group (TG) as they
passed our dingy, grey house on their way to school.

The OTHER Group, (O.G. dem) did pass before THEIR Group
(T.G. dem) but we didn't dare go with O.G. dem to school.
Whenever O.G. dem pass, we use to hide ourselves.
'Hurry, small up ya sef, squeeze down low so O.G. dem
don't see us," we hurry bend down, hide, until O.G. dem pass.

Boys and girls, I-pod- pierced -ears- O.G.- dem was, making noise,
prancing, dancing to the music in their ear-phoned ears, prancing
dancin, comin up slow, but always angry, always in trouble, always
want your money or your lunch or your new things, O.G. dem.

Ear-phoned cords, strangle-wrapped round dey necks, reaching
deep in pockets of brown, blue, black, green, school, skirts and
pants to anchor illegal phones and pads, O.G. dem pants dem
was bottomed off by expensive socks, top of stiff shirts and skirts,
uniforms, nightly embalmed in starch, and steamed crisp daily.

"What wrong wid you bae, try keep still bae, I know ya leg cramp
but I tell you O.G. dem soon pass," O.G. dem, fierce, pierced ears
with gang hairstyle, lookin in our yard to see if they see we to fleece.
O.G. dem mussy smart, they go to school every day without books,
bags, homework, or motivation but O.G. dem always lookin sharp.

O.G. dem strong cuz they draggin everyone, and everything along
with them to 'You Dumb' Bay, located far away from East or West, Bay.
Away from the power found in the House of Bay- Parliament Streets.

Hiding behind the wall, we peep out slow, to make sure O.G. dem gone.
Our leg crampin and tremblin, we stayed low, held in positions
by the memory of that blow mama gave us the last time we show off
and went to school, profilin, letting everybody know we with O.G dem.
"Come out nah, dey gone," my neighbor said, but my brother and I
waited a while, sitting smiling, waiting for the next group, we waited,
drawing circles in the dust, throwing stones at dogs studious in garbage
cans, singing our own ring dance songs until we heard them coming.

"Little Sally water, settle in the saucer, rise Sally, rise, wipe your weeping
eyes ... my brother and me, started singing THEIR Group (T.G. dem) ring
dance song too, we joined them as they passed, safe, hidden, blended
in and lookin and singing like them. They say nothing, we say nothing,
they spare us more pain, we walk in their rhythm, of their song, pretend-
ing to belong, if only for this short journey to our school.

"Chee, Chee, Chee, I am, a pretty lil girl," they laughed, when we
laughed on our steadfast way to school, holding books and homework,
knapped sacked to our backs. Yet why won't they say anything, they
know, we know they know, we know they had us in their sight, when we
were out of sight under cars in their yard, again last night, when border
control police chased my family over walls and searched futilely for us
laying flat under their car mufflers.

I so shame, but I sing the ring dance song anyway, I sing, making sure
my shoulders aren't hunched over, remembering my mother caught in
the impotent dragnet last week, left her strength behind in me, with
instruction to stick with T.G dem (Their Group), sing and clap as they do,
learn to live and walk their path and learn painfully but skillfully to curry
their favor.

Where is God?
(betrayed)

I so sick and tired of people telling me about their God.
I don't want to hear any more about your powerless God.
From what I can see, you'll God and my, suppose Father
ain't never do nuttin to help me.

If my mother sat down and watch someone hurt me
and she didn't do nothing, you people would run jail her.
You'll would try charge her with abuse for neglecting me.
Well you'll need to jail God for neglect because
he sit right down year after year and let me get abused
and did nothing, nothing to help me, jail him!
Jail him because he didn't stop it, and I suppose to forget that?

No chile, your God so awesome he could move mountains,
open up, Red seas, raise up dead people, turn water
into wine, why didn't he do something to help me (suck teeth)

From when I was a little girl going to Sunday school, praying,
I prayed to God to help me and I aint see him do nuttin yet.
Now, I ready to graduate from high school and I still waitin.
So, you need to understand why I aint on your God run.
It does really bug me when people try tell me that I should stop
and ask myself, 'What would Jesus do', I know what Jesus would do.
He would do, what he has always done for me, and that is, nothing.

Well, I am not going to be like Jesus and do nothing, I am going to do
something, if someone need help and I could do it, I ga do it,

they need not ask, I am going to do something, show people that I am
alive and have power see and if anybody run up on me once, they will
never try it twice.

46

I don't play, I'll take out family, anybody who get in my *****way
I soon turn 18 and thanks to your God, I don't have to ever again in life
ask anybody including your God to do anything for me.
He gat enough unanswered request pile up on my file from me.
Any day now he pull my file, he would see that his miracle for me
is past due, I don't owe God anything, he can't get mad with me,
for doing me, I'll take care of myself until you'll God find time
to take care of me, thanks.

Cut Up
(self-harm)

I talk nice,
nobody listens.
I have ideas and
opinions about
what I want
but everybody wants
to control me
all the time.

It's their way
or no other way.
Too many folk
get high bossing
me around.
I cut myself
and watch the
smiles turn
upside down

Cut,
they can't
stop me.
Cut,
it makes me
feel good.
Cut,
I feel powerful
I feel good.

Cut,
Don't get credit
for much but
Cut,
everybody
could see that
Cut,
I have
enough courage
to carve a
bloodline on me
Cut
My Signature
for my control

Part Three: Anti-Self Disorder

A careful look around us will show that some of our children continue to fight the subliminal influences of pigmentocracy. Pigmentocracy encourages investments in narrow, unattainable standards of beauty and femininity. The Cinderella and Snow-White ideals of beauty still strongly influence the acceptance our feminine self-image.

A Skin and A Shame
(pigmentocracy)

You know Miss, is a sin and a shame.   *No*

dark, black- skin gals win this game.   *Black*

girls, with a big nose and thick lip-stick.   *Face.*

down in the bottom, on dis beauty race.   *Here.*

Hold on sister, don't give up so fast!   *Girl*

stop bleach and glow trying to pass.   *Wait!*

Use your head girl, invest in real class.   *Remember*

Character and intelligence beat figure fast.   *Invest!*

Unshackle your mind, slavery still strong.   *Develop!*

Natural beauty, in a class of its own.   *Do Not Self-Hate!*

Stubborn Genes
(bleaching dilemma)

Faithfully bleached,
from the top of
my head, to the
tip of my toe.
How my baby
still come out
so Black?
Man, I really
don't know!
Wanted 'good' hair
long on my back.
I blessed it,
pressed it
It still suck back.
Lord, what I must do?
After all of this,
My hair still picky
And I still black

Weavey-Mae

(weave violence)

Ya weave growlin gal that need a walk!
What you sayin gal, your weave can't talk!
Better lend me that chair Miss from off ya head
I need it to sit down before I dead!

What happen gal, ya weave look beat!
You took Mackey bus and couldn't find seat?
Cheaper I did walk for the trouble I meet.
You see my weave did need 2 extra seats.

Mackey really should a let da matter stand
No. he carryin on, say he is man.
I tell Mackey don't make me run hot,
my weave would take him with a single shot.

Say, get my ugly, gummy weave off he bus,
He doon wan fight, he een wan no fuss,
He is an entrepreneur, doon make him cuss.
Tell me and my weave to get off he bus.

Gal, when I swing my head round,
my weave whap and slap him down.

He grab he pride gal, get up wid bold stand.
Under bus seat, back wid cutlass in he hand.
Wid all he might, he swing at weave.
Gal she bend over and roll up she sleeve.

My weave gal, she had him by he neck
Tear up all he bus seat, a fight to the death.
Up from da floor, Mac try run for da door.
All dat weave- glue gal, she nail him to da floor.

Blind him wit she colour, she reel dat man in.
Dust take he breath gal and odour take he wind.
Nuff respect you'll, for dem 1000-piece sew in.
Weave had Mac beggin forgiveness for he sins

Now Mac is a humble man, he does learn fast
Lemme go gal, I een ga last, you bad gal,
weave you win, take two extra seat gal
whenever you and ya owner come in.

Raisin Leg

(Prejudice: true incident of a young lady insulted by a neighbour who
didn't like her clothes and attributed her dress to sexual motives)

"Lil girl go home
and cover up ya hip.
Put on underwear,
and sew up that split.
Stand up straight
to hide ya crease.
Everywhere you sit
you leaving streak.
Jelly, raisin thighs,
rubbing, giving off heat.
You scratchin in public
like you gat flea.
It really hard for
people to tell,
if ya trying to
catch man or
you tryin to sell.
With the bait
you using, the most
you ga see,
is a left over
beating and
full HIV."

Part Four: Hypocritical Social Images

Some of the decisions made by adults can contribute to our children becoming prematurely sexualized, amoral, defiant of authority, distracted and derailed long before other more positive characteristics have had a chance to develop. For example, the structure and function of some of our households expose children prematurely to a level of sexual activity that is inappropriate for their ages. While some adults responsibly teach low risk behavior, there are some households that may inadvertently support risky behaviour. As an example, in a household, there may be a child there who is three years old, whose mother is 15, the grandmother is 26, and the great-grandmother is 39. Mother, grandmother, great-grandmother and all of the other adolescents and adults in the home may be sexually active. Their partners may all come to visit or live in the small home. These children at an early age can become used to these male or female partners stepping over them on the floor through the night or early mornings. So inadvertently, their mornings can begin with a sexual reference and the night can also end with one.

What is even more disconcerting is that in some situations, the partners are <u>not ashamed</u> to be stepping over the children on the floor. Worse, the resident- parent <u>may not be upset</u> that the visiting partner can so comfortably step over the children on the floor on the way to the one bedroom. The situation descends to a new level of chaos, when the visiting partner is allowed or encouraged to deprive the children of their food, toiletries, and or items of clothing. Energy is expended to ensure the adult's comfort. It can be heartbreaking to hear stories of children who come to school after having had the last piece of soap, the last piece of bread, or their clean school shirt used by a visitor.

In addition to these situations, we have adult models of substance abuse, chronic lying, and patterns of violent and disorderly behavior. These social models are at times accompanied by verbal messages encouraging youth to 'do as I say and not as I do'. At other times, we find pockets of what could be called cultural psychopathy, the level of which could be almost unbelievable. An adult can stand up in the front of a group of children and say, 'Why these "F…in" children don't stop cursing? I don't know what's wrong with them. If any of my children cursed in my hearing, I would slap the '****'' out of them." Another incident, " I don't know why my neighbor upset. My family ran a yellow drop (extension) cord from his outdoor socket when he wasn't home, what's the problem, at least we didn't break into his house and thief his money like some common robber. Another example, " The man had sex with a teenage girl, that doesn't mean that he is not decent at least he did not kill her…nobody perfect, don't judge.

Subcultural Differences

In a funeral in a protestant church in the middle of a crowded urban neighborhood, women and men in conservative suits sit next to teenagers and adults dressed in peeping (private parts can be peeped) black shorts which are indistinguishable from underwear. There are some with figure hugging spandex tights in lieu of trousers, balanced on stiletto heels with the picture of the deceased on snug t-shirts. Young men hang around the church yard with undisguised alcoholic beverages and some smoke marijuana, the scent of which wafts through the open church windows. The deceased had been found bound and gagged and shot in the back of his head. The preacher while doing his "dust to dust" rite called out for non-violence and a decrease in the crime rate, especially armed robbery. One of the 'soldiers' in the audience hollered back…'If ya don't have it, take it by any means necessary and let the strong survive daddy'…and his supporters gave him a shout-out and a solid round of applause.

In the graveyard processional, young girls gyrate over open rum bottles to the sound of the band as the casket is taken into the grave site. Young men wrestle for an opportunity to be pall bearers for the known 'bad man' as he is transported to his final resting place. Meanwhile, baby mamas of the deceased, all holding their offspring, are at verbal war, right under the tent in front of the grave where the wife and other children of the deceased are sitting. Family members of the deceased are making loud references to the crocodile tears of the estranged wife now sitting in the front of the obviously hostile relatives.

Just when you thought it could not become worse, war broke out in the graveyard with enough violence and cursing to raise the dead. Those in funeral finery disputed with the bottle top dancers. Yet as the police escorted attendants from the cemetery, with guns drawn, many at the funeral shook their heads in confusion, wondering where did all this violence and societal mayhem come from.

The voices below reflect the hypocritical vortex in which some of our children are immersed.

Stop Lyin'
(dreams adults sell)

"Class, you can be anything
you want to be!"
"Teacher, stop lyin!"
"Age ain't nothin but a number!"
"You lyin still!"
"The sky is the limit!"
"Listen to them spin it!"
Yet the biggest lie though,
"You reap what you sow!"

"Big people, you'll lyin though!
Peep in *my* window, me, 5th of
eight children in a house for two
waiting my turn, for change due
from the 150 a week left after insurance
and my mudda numbers and A-sue

150 to share for bus fare, light and
rent due, lunch, without-breakfast,
dinner too, come teacher, do put
your fancy foot in my disadvantaged shoe.
Be anything I want to be, right!
My mama have a new man of
no land, no job, no paper, but money
for gold teet, and the latest Nike.

Reapin what *we* sow, stop lyin!
I reapin what *they* sow, that is disadvantage
in my life where Education Loans and
scholarships are for advantaged friends
with money not eaten by bus fare or fear
Not for children from poor schools at all.
Students like me can clearly see
you'll grown folks just plain, lyin.

Disadvantage sewn in my life
without 40 dollars for school skirt or
30 dollars for shirt without neck tie.
Twenty dollars a week for snack -lunch
without healthy drink or calorie count.
Tell the lie to children with no long
morning rides on expensive, loud- buses
driving to confused schools not looking
inside me to see what I can be if
I don't get that two point zero.

The sky is the limit?
Teacher, please, stop lyin!
Look, Tatlantis and Bar-Ma,
the glass ceilings for all a we
we even us with B.G.C.S.E,
even us with unpaid loan Degree.
Someone, please check this hypocrisy!
Reap what we sow, all these lies and
That lies, all must go, the truth is
It is us who weepin, reapin, sunk deep
in disadvantages our adults sow and sew.

Poison Conch Salad

(Serial Polygamy 'outside' children)

One full sister, and one full brother, of my daddy and my mother, live with my daddy-mother, on the eastern side of Johnson Rd, and the one half- brother, of my lovely mother, live with he daddy, near the old, red church in the Grove.

I sorry for my *oldest* half-sister, also from my mother, who lived with the girlfriend- of- mother's- half- brother; my oldest -half-sister moved back in with her ex, cause *girlfriend* -of- mother's- half -brother, put my oldest half-sister's boyfriend out.

Now my *youngest* half -sister- daddy, does work to the chicken shack, he is a good help because when he bring food for my youngest half-sister, is be nuff to eat and pack, but mother new- boyfriend Pat, say he stoppin dat, no other man bringin food in this house behind he back.

My mother new- boyfriend- old- girlfriend's *other* children daddy, does give his chirren lunch, but if my mother new- boyfriend- old -girlfriend, wan feed the chirrin she had with him, she does sell weed, newspaper and ask the school to give them lunch.

My 2 half-brothers, from my father, live in Fox Hill by the tree stump, I see them all the time on my way to the water pump, now my 2 half-brothers of my father, they go to private school, they fees pay, but father, for us the children with my mother, he always broke, he live playing the fool.

Mother say next time he here, have no fear she will mark him with edge tool, but my father not fool, he drivin sweetheart jeep, busy takin my half-brother dem to private school, mother een ga ketch him nah, he too busy showing the jeep off, being Mr. Cool.

But my mother say not to worry bout a ting, my daddy and his sweet-heart won't go far, my father only with she, long as he could drive her new car, the first time he can't afford gas and payment for da jeep, he'll be right back round here lookin for place to sleep

Before I have children, there is no doubt, I must call a family reunion to straighten my bloodline out, I don't know what this thing is about, why can't parents have all their children in the same family, in the same house?

Amen Mamas

(maternal hypocrisy)

Saved, sanctified doing the work of the Lord.
Move that '****' shirt off my new iron board!
Holy, shoutin, serious, Bible readin too.
"Boy get your *****.up, clean ya *** shoe!'

Pink satellite hat, pearls with matchin shoe,
dress to kill every church-day sittin in special pew,
We motto is: Do as we say and not what we do.

Show respect, Rev.on ZNX, boy he look clean!
Quick write da prayer line number off dat screen.
Buyin five piece a dat tomorra from Hitian Jean.
Prayer meeting tomorra night, make sure ya clean,

Girl, remind ya man after he reach to lock da gate.
If ya hook up and watchin new XXX on DVD,
Close ya door so ya chirren can't hear and see.

Let him carry back dem old XXX on the floor,
I finish dem, tell him bring me some more.
If the rent man call, play like ya een hear.
Stay out he way, een no money to give here.

If he ketch ya, look in he eye, say I een home,
I'll be in prayer, takin my cares before da throne.
He rent is seed money today, down payment for
ma well deserved blessins for which I done pray.

Saturday Night Live

(domestic insanity)

My father swing the cutlass at my mother.
She stepped to the side, bringing out she lye.
" Swing dat cutlass again, round dis place,
I'll splash dis whole jar of acid in ya ogly face!"
"Oh stand dere gal if ya tink ya bad,
I throwin you and ya chirren out ma yard!"

Out da window came some of our clothes.
Out da back door, he push we oil stove.
" You throwin my things in the yard?
You know I is da best woman you ever had."
Ma take out she match and she did scratch,
lighting flame, for the ole house to catch.

Daddy lick da match from out she hand.
Dem two was wrestling all over the ground.
Ma get up first, and cut him thru he shirt
He stab her wid the fork, den fling her in da dirt.
Out come mama foot, she trip him to the ground.
All our neighbours dem done gather round.

Daddy jump up and pushed mammy down.
3 slaps cross her face, stomp her waist,
2 more kicks to the side, he spit in her eye.
Mamma rolled over and was still, still.
Daddy reach down and wipe he wet eyes.
Sheila! Sheila! Sheila, baby, open ya eye.
I love you so much sweets, please don't die!

Mamma reach up, and try to grab daddy hair.
Daddy jump up, start sprinting in the air.
What you'll lookin at, find something to do.
Iron clothes, wash the dishes, clean shoes.
Tell ya pa hurry up come eat he food,
Let me carry him to the outpatient unit
of the hospital while I in a good mood.

Part Five: Sexual Violence

The status of sexual violence in the Bahamas is covered in more detail in the book, *Without Consent: Without Intent* the companion text to this publication.

The Impact of Sexual Violence on Children
1. Betrayal Anger
The child can experience betrayal anger when the nature of their victimization becomes clear to them. The understanding that "the person who I thought valued me and was protecting me, is the person who became comfortable violating me" may evoke feelings of anger, loss, worthlessness, and disillusionment and overwhelm the child.

Traumatic Sexualization
Children, who have been raped, molested or experienced sexual violence in any kind of way can come to view their bodies as objects, their greatest tool for negotiating business and interpersonal transactions. They may use sex to search for love and attachment.

Graphic Imagery Recall
Sometimes, during the act or course of molestation, images of pain, force, humiliation, loss of personal power, and sense of control are combined with feelings of defeat, subjugation, disloyalty, and betrayal. These can be absorbed by the children. Flashbacks maybe experienced.

Mind Bending
The mental trauma of not being believed is sometimes as intense as the trauma of being believed. Being believed destroys families, friendships, and can result in the imprisonment of a valued family member or friend. This is a large burden to add to the ongoing trauma. The mind-bending trauma of an official investigation can be a source of further devastation

Stigmatization
If victims of abuse come to perceive themselves as "ruined" or "spoiled" in some irreparable way, they may carry that stigma with them for a lifetime. They may live experiencing a sense of "difference," understanding that something that has happened to them has not happened to other people.

Learned Helplessness
Upon evaluating the dynamics of molestation where the children initially fought psychologically or physically to ward off violation but were unsuccessful, they may believe that fighting off a predator or reporting the matter is forever useless because nothing can be done to stop the abuse.

Sexualization
A young woman's sense of worth has become rooted in her sex appeal (I am nothing if I can't arouse men). No other skill, personality trait or characteristic is more important than her sex appeal. Energy goes into perfecting the art/science of gaining the attention of members of the opposite sex well beyond the level expected for others her age.

The voices below are that of young people coping with sexual violence i.e. incest, gang rape, abortion, acquaintance rape, infanticide, statutory rape, sexual harassment. All of the stories here except one are stories told by Bahamian children. One of the stories was adjusted to include details of a similar story of another youth in another part of the Caribbean. This was done to make it impossible to identify the story teller because her case was so widely reported in the media. The final format tells her story while hiding her identity.

Let It Rest

(Father Incest : victim's narrative: a true story)

When my friends raped me,
it did hurt me really bad.
Bleed, but didn't breed,
angry, scared, shame, sad.
Didn't tell nobody either,
didn't want dem call me "bad."
People always told me 'bout
dem friends I use to have.
For a long time, had it on the
shelf, nobody to blame,
     blamed me
     blamed myself.

But when my daddy raped
me, seventh time, drunk
on da floor, i screamed in
and outside me, Lord,
i can't take much more,
what to do, he cried so hard
"Don't call da police baby"
tears, cries, rum, please.
"Each time, I pray, God
does forgive me, won't you
     forgive me too,
     forgive me, please?"

My family for true did have
so much stress, i laid my head
on my pillow and let it rest till
one girl at school cross me and
i open her arm with one deep
slice, fooled by hidden stress,
i thought i had put my
hurt to bed, had taken the
pain off my chest off
                my chest!!!
                My Chest.

Incarcerated, detained i thought i had it together
                i thought i had let it rest.

Interview in Bed

(sexual harassment: a real experience)

Who will be hired today?

Sitting within polished
office view,
waiting for my interview,
dressed for success,
graduations' best,
copies of degrees
neatly tucked in folder
on my knees,
professionalism,
at ease

In comes the boss,
distinguished head
tossed, with a calm,
'good morning' bow.
Then, a sad, old man,
mop in hand, said,
"friend, you have
paper all well and good.
but I will give you
a hunch, the only girl
getting hired today
is the one who
gives up, the boss
man's 'lunch!'

Waiting for my interview,
dressed for success,
graduations' best,
copies of degrees
neatly tucked in folder
on my knees,
professionalism,
killed by this
rampant disease

I Need to Bleed

(step-father incest : victim narrative of transactional incest: real story)

Please Lord let me bleed; I can't carry this seed within me.
There's no space for a little face among the dreams and
    hopes mommy invested in me,

Mommy's life on hold, her sacrifices for me taking their toll,
I need to bleed, to have time to grow the seed for the better
    future she willed, and planted in me.

Have mercy on my soul, this scared, fourteen years old,
I need courage not to hide the name of my Step Pappy.
    my monthly bleed, for Mama please,

She thanks You every night for Step Pappy, she'll die if the seed
of his incestuous deed, grows uninterrupted nine months within
    me Let me bleed, please,
to hide his need for repayment for education, food and money.

Your Ho'

(teenager trapped in prostitution: real story)

Listen how you name me; clothed, how you framed me, busy at what
you taught me; sitting where you left me
My shoe, now heavy on your foot.

Firsthand knowledge, earning rent, sex didn't require legal consent,
nakedness no longer needs the dark; no condom purchased for my
heart.
My shoe, now heavy on your foot;

69 not always a number; "sleep with" didn't always have slumber,"juicin"
didn't always need fruit; didn't need all that pain in my youth.
My shoe, now heavy on your foot

'Balls' not always with bat; sometimes raincoat without hat,
"doggies" didn't all have fleas; there was no pleasure on my knees
My shoe, now heavy on your foot

Rape didn't always call police, sadly not only parents beat, pain, invisible,
running deep; no discretion now with whom I "sleep", walk a mile, please
In my shoe now heavy on your feet.

Listen how you judge me! clothed in what you bought me
busy at what they pay me; sitting where they displaced me
A mile, in my shoe, now heavy on their foot.

Listen how they name you; hear them publicly defame you
And me I do blame you; Hope I publicly shame you
For these shoes, now heavy on my foot

My Baby Daddy Name

(teenager's proud reflection on statutory rape: true account)

He say don't tell you'll his name, you'll will try jailing him, giving him
the blame.
Though he call me first, is me who gone to him, using my own mind and
yes it's a sin.
Don't ask me again and no I ain't shame, I will not tell you, my baby
daddy name.

He 34, he know my age, fourteen in couple a days, yes I go to his house
out west.
Only out there, I could get some rest, home for me is cursing, poverty
and pain
yes he been to jail twice, I ain't shame, I still ain't tellin you'll my baby
daddy name.

I know he married and yes, I ain't he wife, stay out my business Ms. and
get ya own life.
He listens when I talk, yes he buy me things, but I have the man, and you
have da rings.
Yeah I use he cell, use he ATM too, but my baby daddy name gat nuttin
ta do with you.

True Mam, I is number two, but from what I hear, wish I could say the
same about you.
No attitude mam, tellin it like it is, this the way to play mam, take the
Bahamian quiz.
Who you know ain't have baby, don't takes dates, money and tings
from man?

How much man with degree want be with a girl like me, least dis man
        tries to please me.
Who gat man with one woman, who gat a holy man, with manners and a
        savings plan?
Don't judge my good man, I know where he stand, half a you'll talkin
        gat she-he man

Remember he say don't tell you'll his name, you'll will try jail him, give
        him the blame.
Though he call me first, is me who gone to him, using my own mind, and
        yes it's a sin.
Don't ask me again and no I ain't shame, I will not tell you, my baby
        daddy name.

Gang Rape

I had a date for quarter past four,
dressed like grown up people me
and Rico walked through the door,
man at the desk ask for ID, my Rico
slipped him a cool hundred and 50;
happy that my man really love with me

We went quietly to the second floor;
Rico was right for me, I was so sure;
Comfortable with him behind this door;
then came a small knock; I wasn't scared.
Smart Rico hide my clothes off the bed.
Under the blanket so no one could see,
Rico let in four friends to my surprise party,

Didn't know what to do trapped, shocked,
Rico looked like this was nothing new;
hand over my mouth, holdin down my head,
feet held firmly to my once secure bed
Soul and trust flowed in oceans of tears,
body violated, eyes open, inside dead.

Rico say een no ting, his friends share erry ting,
but I can't tell anyone bout this thing, because
I don't want add murder to this ting
Rico can't get why he can't still be my man,
I tell him train ain't part a my datin plan.

On the road his friends dey call me sexy.
Say out loud how much they respect me, say
ain't much girls alive could pull dey train of five.
I sit down sadly, dead, shamed, in my class.
This obstacle Lord, how will it pass?
I can't sleep at night, its heavy on my mind,

Am I a ho' now? No, I will be fine; fine
how can that be? I wonder if I have HIV,
what about pregnancy, and my dance ministry?
I can't believe Rico do this to me,
ga ta study for test in Chemistry, test for HIV,
test for baby, test for the fighter in me.

Abortion

(abortion by another name: A true story)

My pretty ma tired beat me from round my boyfriend door; without
shame, pretty me, go back, each day, afterschool for more; she say my
man old enough to be her man, one day she may even try her hand, she
say "stay from round dat man, stay out he car, stop drinkin' wid him in
da corner bar, you only 13 girl is a sin to see, how you lettin' da man get
ya tings for free, make sure he wrap it up, so you don't ketch disease, I
don't want nuttin destroy my sweet life of ease.'

The 14th of the month must be an important date, my man always
checkin' to see if Red- water late; don't worry, you could be sure, on the
14, Red-water always came knockin' at the front door; the first time my
man didn't see Red-water run, he get scared, say free-stylin' done; he
has to get a good protection plan; must show respect for dat Red-water
man; Reds must come once a month ya see, so my boyfriend-man could
stay jail- free, he must stay free to take care of me.

I couldn't understand this weird thing you see, Red-water was more
important than me; every second week of the four, boyfriend must
check the front door; when one day Red-water was late, boyfriend gone
crazy, starin' at the gate; sayin' he must "catch' the horse because it
done leave the gate; he need to do the thing before it too late"; what
horse, what gate, what thing, what late; someone need to explain this
strange meal on my confused plate!

My boyfriend buy this funny stick-ting, made me pee in a cup, and
wait for a blue ring; blue ring came, how fast things changed; he slap
my face say pretty gal ga cause him big disgrace; boyfriend gone crazy,
he actin' strange; 'things' he says must change, 800 dollars, phone card,
doctor phone number, I must carry these to my pretty mother; I thought
I did catch dat disease what mama did dread, I take dem tings and put

dem under my bed, I sick, vomitin' and scared, thinking I have HIV, I mussy ga dead.

My ma suddenly take notice, I was broke, not pretty and not cute, 'what happen gal why you look sick', I tell her bout the Red-water, cup and blue ring on the lil' stick; whap, one back hand slap, two licks wid one shoe, she broke up the fan while smashin' up dishes and flingin' da fryin' pan too; how come I never tell her I did not see the Red-water-man; you pregnant gal dats for sure, but no baby comin' through that young door, with my hair in she hand, we went to find my man.

When we get in front he house, she took her stand, with big stick in hand she started to shout, "Bring your black you know what out," as one other lil' pretty neighbour girl come runnin' out he door; boyfriend come out smiling, half- dressed in shame, what he was smiling bout I wasn't sure; my ma grip him, body slam him on the floor; I watch mother all through the fight, beat him bad, wonderin' why it took her so long to make things right.

It was strange to see, it look like she really did care bout me, when I look, she was holdin he pants' waist and breathin' rum down he face, "I want money and I want it now, sell dem gold teet, sell ya car, my brudda if you tink it funny, come back round here without dat money; no one explained nothing to me; I told her about da money I hide from she, the money he done did give me; not to worry she said I would see, she will get a doctor to take the disease-ring out my pee.

"Just do what the doctor say and da problem would go away"; they that the doctor could bring, Red-water and prettiness back to me; if Red-water came back to me, things would return to how they use to be; just as planned, taken to doctor- man, and my red-water man came back to me; weeks later all is well, I hear the school bell, must hurry and not be late; yet somethin' in my mind just ain't fine as mother again tried to explain this thing to me:

"When ya Red-water came down, I was wrong, about there being a baby there ya see; the blue ring on the stick was a little trick, to see if you was disease free, the doctor did give you a Vitamin see, to stop Red-water turnin' to a real baby; mother had no fear, boyfriend was clear, said I would be straight soon with money too; one day in school chair, it all became clear when Tru' Gossip sat close to my ear, say she hear, my abortion clear, but don't fear, cuz she been there..here.. too.

Baby Gone
(throwing baby away at birth)

12 years old and only know fun. Never been taught about how life begun. Father lost and Mother dead, living with great grandmother instead. Grammie lived in house on hill top. Never much to eat, no place to shop. Clothes were always hand me downs, but I was well loved by people all around. My half blind grammie took good care of me. Didn't have gas stove or electricity, just an old lamp, not much space, I loved the house, school, wide, clean open place.

Stomach start growing funny. I felt a little bump but I was never worried, I was never plump. Breast became bigger, people said I was growing up. It didn't bother me when some time I threw up. Months passed, couldn't stay wake in class, Teacher thought I was sick and she let it pass. I never worried. I didn't get plump. Then one day the bump moved and I began to holler, I began to scream. People came running, thought I was funnin, I was so spooked and so shame. Dey say I haunted, ghost callin my name; Started wearing big clothes and stopped sleepin in school. Sat down under the tree and watched the bump move. Oh my God what spell is this that could make my belly move? Did my gremmie fix me, I wasn't rude? My mother died long ago tell me is this she? I need to find out now before I go crazy. I sat and wondered, I had to find my head. Maybe I was dying. Maybe I was dead. I sat watching my belly in dread, till an idea came in my head. My belly look like Miss Jennie own and Miss Jennie had a baby and now it home.

I only a little girl and Miss Jennie, she was full grown. Only big woman could have baby, that was known. I sat under the tree looking at my belly hard as stone. Lord if I havin a baby, please, let me die. This would kill my grandmother, only on me she relies. Was I having a baby? I never found out, I just kept on going knowing that one day it would come out; school over for summer early that help me out, could hide my stomach now small but stout.

My stomach move often but I never made a face. My grammy knew nothing, I stayed out her space, always smiling, my calm face; one morning I got up and noticed I was wet. I did nothing. It was summer I thought it was sweat. My stomach started hurtin, but it didn't last. I went on doing my work hopin it would pass. I went and lay down in the field for the rest of the day. Every time a pain came, I cried and I pray. As it was getting late, grammie came to call me in. 'I goin over to Aunt Georgie', another lie another sin.

When it became dark, I slowly walked home, sneaked into the back room and lay down near the broom; When the pain hit me, I put the towel in mouth. This way I could stop the scream from coming out. I blew out the lamp so I could pretend to sleep. I screamed with the pillow over my head and the towel in my teeth. Early the next morning with the wet towel round my mouth, with one last push the bump and all the bloody things came out.

Without looking, I ball up everything in the sheet. I stepped into darkness and slowly crossed the street. Bump started makin noise and I started to run, I roll the whole sheet down over the hill and came back home me one. I lay back down tired and I went to sleep. I got up early and washed all the sheets. I scrubbed the floors and made everything neat. I went and talked to mama after making her tea. I went back in the bed and went straight to sleep.

When I got up there was commotion in the streets, they had found a baby in the bush near the bottom of the hill. It was in the hospital and it was living still. Grammie shook her head, dese young girls was a shame. She said it was the parents who should take the blame. Next day inspectors came a knockin, knockin at every door, want know if we know anything. Not me, for sure. They wanted all young girls to the hospital for a check. I went with the crowd. They won't catch me I would bet.

I was feeling nothing. I wasn't even scared. I didn't have a baby. I had a bump instead. When nurse done check me, she slowly shook her head. She said 'lil girl tell me, why you want ya baby dead?' Shock slap me upside my head. I een had no baby miss, I was scared, I thought I was ga dead; tings wasn't right in my head, don't bring da bump back to me, this time, I ain't scared, I'll cut it up and make sure it dead.

Baby is Money: Violations of the Mind

Over the years, there were many memorable individual and group conversations with insightful children and youth. The observations below reflect segments of an unplanned youth-centered discourse about teenage pregnancy. The group was comprised of girls and boys between thirteen and seventeen years of age. The impression gleaned from listening to that conversation was that 'baby' and 'pregnancy' could have the same value as money and the pregnancy was God's doing.

> Miss is not every time you see a girl pregnant means she
> plan it ya know! You know you may go out with a dude and
> ya just get caught up. Sometimes it does be an accident
> but I don't really believe anything is ever an accident. If God
> didn't want that baby to come, he would have stopped it.
> So, in a way it was an accident but not really an accident.

Some girls would have allowed pregnancy if they believed that the father would provide them with financial support for the baby and money for themselves. In those circumstances having a baby was similar to finding a job. As to what could convince a girl that a young unemployed man was able to support a child and its mother, it was understood that part of the game of persuasion involved promising the impossible. The young man's promise- the- impossible message had to be framed properly with the right degree of romantic overtures. If the girl was emotionally needy to the right degree, then the chances of getting a positive response was significantly increased. If the message was not getting through fast enough, applying a little physical pressure to go with the message was acceptable.

However, for many of the boys they would have been happy if they had become a father at a young age. The respect they would have earned would be something that money could not pay for. Baby, was the visible proof that a young man was not homosexual. So, getting a baby-disclaimer in early was worth the price. No career or clothes or any other achievement in life was able to provide this disclaiming service. This was an important service because any suggestion of homosexuality was met with scorn, derision and even physical violence.

For some girls, 'baby' was an eternal signature that they had been desired by somebody. This was especially important if the girl's social status was low, and there was a prevailing perception that she could never persuade anybody to be intimate with her. Becoming pregnant would prove them wrong. There were some comments that even suggested that the value of a woman is influenced more by 'baby' than by any other material possession (house, lot, car, degree, money).

Part Six: Empowerment

Our children need empowering. They struggle with so many challenges. Childhood role reversal, role strain, boundary collapses, premature sexualization, premature aging, adults behaving like children, all threaten their childhood. There are so many angry children in need of restored childhood and solace.

One fierce challenge is Parentification. Parentification is the official term used to describe family patterns, where at the expense of their own childhood, children and adolescents function as adults. They experience roles with responsibilities normally expected of adults in a given society. A child who has been parentified does not mentally differentiate between adulthood and childhood. Having assumed too large caretaking roles from an early age, (paying bills, caring for their own needs, needs of siblings, friends, relatives, parents, fighting off predators or coping with trauma), they cannot perceive that there are any adult behaviors that are off limits to them alcohol, drugs and sex, driving included. They've been asked to function as adults all of their young lives. Age restrictions are immaterial.

As an extension of this when they do grow into legal adulthood, this dysfunctional perception of childhood continues. They behave with children the way they should behave with their peers. There is nothing they would not ask or expect a child to do. There is no understanding that there are needs or behaviors specific to certain ages. A female is a woman and fair game no matter how old she is, same with males. This opens the door for abuse and exploitation.

In times of economic downturn, children and adolescents are more vulnerable to exploitation, parentified children being the most vulnerable of the lot. They feel the adult weight of the crisis. They will be exploited by those legal adults out there who have few restrictions if any about what should or should not be offered or demanded in exchange for resources to make ends meet.

The voices below reflect struggles with aspects of Bahamian realities that could threaten personal stability.

Sister Degree
(Gender)

Sister Degree, prostrated,
black- sun- sand- sea- symbol.
Weaved, bleached, nailed,
to mattresses buried in
clapboard and cement.
Placed in token envelopes
addressed to Equality.
Her Degree vain in front of
tribes-people fixated on baby,
and man, where worth of
warriors and maidens grow
in serial polygamy, misogyny
mammies *and man*;

no need for a Brother's Degree
if Sister-with- Degree, and
mammies give ride and place
to warriors unfettered of
mortgage, pride and
commitment and money.

"Is we tribal way", dey say.
"Came from slavery by whitey,
colonial, imperialists dem man!"
Baby is contentment, and, man.
The plan that makes we complete.
Intellectual stimulation…Elite.
Degree a legitimate substitute
for coitus stimulation incomplete.

Woman-content-man content
woman don't need no Degree;
don't need no plan, just a man

Sister with Degree what is her fate,
if she wants to not participate,
or procreate, vegetate, fornicate?
She must educate in legitimate
Substitution for placement on
mattresses interred in clapboard
and cement in token envelopes
addressed to Money, Inequality,
Vanity, Dependent-Masculinity
and Denied- Citizenship.

My Virginity

(destructive guest speakers)

Guest Speaker, cool, well dressed,
educated, enthused, asked classmates
what kind of birth control they used.
As she went around the class,
it got to be my turn at last.
She repeated the question, all laughed,
'She is the only virgin left in this class'.
Speaker question, 'You're a virgin?'
You don't have to be shame,
Ain't no blame, ain't no sin, false pride,
No need to hide that you already gave in.'

It finally cut me, this hypocrisy
this audacity, I can't just let it win!
What kind of Christian nation I live in!
I have to apologize for being a virgin!
People treat me like I have a disease.
Around me they lose respect and their ease.
"You tink you better than people eh?
You know what, I really think you gay.
You'll funny people should from round me stay."
Nation screams out to put violence on hold.
But for sex, they don't expect same self-control.

"It's your nature," dey quick to say,
"Solomon had plenty partners in his day.
God understands, Him make you dat way."
If a virgin I want to be, please let me be!
Why does this Christian nation persecute me?

Not because <u>your</u> impulse you didn't control,
Should you assume I couldn't be that bold!
In this Christian nation, virginity is my right!
Excuse me mam, please, get this thing right.
Instead of discouragin me, help me fight!
If I delay, support me, don't get uptight!
In this Christian nation, virginity is my right!

"Use protection when we play", you say,
How about debate, beach, camping, pray
for strength to fight when urges get strong?
Nothing bad about using the word 'wrong.'
Respect the different values in this room!
Leave misinformation and prejudice at home!
When you come before people to present,
include 'Wait', Bible Protection 100%.
Please forgive me mam, I just had to vent.

Male Alienation

Cunning, marauding oceans
ferry 'Abused Human Rights
Cruise' wailing, flailing along.
Guarding below deck and standard,
precious, gold, black cream of crop.
shackled, yet free, entrenched in stench
of proud African manhood-fatherhood
congealed in waste to the waist,
surviving
the Middle Passage
To
Nowhere.

Castrating nightmares soil my bed.
My 'Can't-marry' wife embraced,
swollen, legitimately placed
in Massa's lewd waist and zipper.
Legal lynching pens strip and whip
my children's mind of family.
Thousands born, torn, inspected,
gone, untitled, to bleed and breed
in haste through
his Middle Passage
to
Nowhere.

1848-Abolition-Deceit screamed 'Freed'
to roam for my children.
Fear! Hold Still Fear!
Must position my face in Time and Space

so my children could see me, recognize me,
respect I for their legacy survives in me
their carefully guarded Title to
a path out of this emerging journey
to
Nowhere

The 1900s, freed feet touch land but quick sand.
Her Majesty's bonds arrive to greet me.
Quick! I and I drop, roll, disguising I Title,
Hiding I soul, hoping my people
still recognize me.
Signaling my children, I must flee
Union Jack's wedding to UBP.
No legitimate voice or seat yet for me
at The Table
to
Somewhere

1973-Awe! Whash-ga lash! Brigga-Dum-Bam!
Mace-fling lickin' Burma Road Drum.
Title Erupt-Us! Democracy rushin' scrap!
Quiet-bloodless- revolution shaking silver bells
and Spoons from Mouths,
and biting, bandaging Her Majesty's food-hand
that painfully.
rises from The Table in futile haste
trying to chase gold, black crop
back in place
in the Middle Passage
to
Nowhere.

The 2000s, are crystal-clear oceans
where I watch my now Titled, black Boys
with full decks, fat and large at The Table.
playing with paying debts to a people
long owed three Aces and a King.
Pulling lawyer MAN
and vendor MAN with fender
up in dozens from grassroots floor
while families cheer, share prayer
WITHOUT care
for their Title
to
Somewhere

Free elections, loaded Deck and Dice,
my children put Ingraham in game with Flame
for Pingdom, as Perry-Ping was scorched
with Flamin' Torch for banking on church
tongue and good intention.
Listen what's that, I hear
see and fear,
years of prison-bus sirens
screaming
'Captured Greed',
sirens again screaming
pulling political sheep
from mental sleep, slipping
into the Middle Passage
to
Nowhere

Every morning, God Almighty it can't be real,
four prison bus loads packed with sons black,
the golden cream of our legacy crop,
going dislocated, to Her Majesty
Slop and trap
for pretty shoes
and piece
with no skill or
mortgage money.
Going full speed
to
Nowhere

These are MY Children, why aren't they yet free
Hold still rage, must position my face
where Justice can see me,
recognize me
and insist that
Every black **M**ale-**A**frican-**N**emesis
find a way to rescue these children
from this
Rite-of-Passage
to
Nowhere.

My Children Bay Street Brothers
with pretty shoes
and piece, sip Parliament-brew
in view of baby-daddies
without fathers, entrenched,
in waste in the Middle Passage
of that Fig Tree, and Nassau Court Street,

where Gender-Benders plea for
'Innocent Boys'
"Set him free, my good boy, he adores me."
With me he will go fast
to
Nowhere

'Won't- Marry' wives bleached-aglow,
Wear SUVs and condos tied to public g-strings.
"Yes, I Single Sir, 3 jobs Sir.
Where he daddy Sir?
He ga be a little late,
He out workin' on 'Three Straight.'
But set my-boy free. Sir
So I
could tie him
to me
And I'll
make sure
Sir
that he
go
Nowhere."

Still I Rise

(Maya Angelou Adapted by a group of young ladies)

You try to tear me up with your bitter words
try to stamp me down in the dirt
But see…Still I rise

My intelligence seems to upset you
Why you so full of gloom because I walk
With pride running through my bones?

Just like the moons and like the suns
And the sureness of the tides, my hopes
spring high because whether you like it or not
Look out…here I rise.

Oh! Did you want to see me broken.
bowed head and lowered eyes,
shoulders falling, wet with tear drops
weakened by my soulful cries
Sorry, 'cause still..I rise,

Don't let my deep self-respect offend you
Don't take it so hard that I hold my head high.
In the midst of all my trouble
See I still rise.

You may shoot me with your jealousy
Cut me with your eyes, try killing me with
Your hatefulness…but look out
'cause still…I rise

Does my sophisticated manner offend you?
Does it come as a surprise, that I don't
give out my body as a cheap, easy prize?
Out of the hurts of yesterday's shame,
I rise up from a past, rooted in pain.

I rise a young Bahamian woman
leaping excelling, I want to break free.
without fear of failing, free to be me.
Into a new daybreak so wonderfully clear
I rise!

Bringing the gifts that so many people gave me.
I am their dream, I am their hope. I am me.
Watch me rise, I rise. I rise.
Still I rise.

Part Seven: How to Help.

Self- Awareness/ Mindfulness Training

Intervention activities should bring children in touch with their feelings. This will allow for deliberate efforts to manage these feelings. They can be helped to understand how the emotional currents from their negative life experiences affect their learning and behavior. Some children need help to manage the complex social relationships evolving from the many persons trafficking through their lives on a daily basis. Some need help to identify and confront internalized negative belief systems about learning, sexuality, violence, beauty etc. Others need help to identify and understand how these negative belief systems affect their growth and development.

Self-Management Training

Skills can be taught for managing emotional surges. Activities should target negative thoughts and show how these affect feelings and behavior. Peers can be used to help. For adolescents who do not experience debilitating, dislocating life events, these ones can be taught to recognize 'power shortages' in their peers. Awareness of such can help them to react to their challenged-peers in a manner that could prevent an 'electrical blow out' (extended conflicts). Other interventions by properly trained personnel can help with self-doubts, discouragement, diminished self-esteem, and apathy.

The expressions in this section offer suggestions on how adults can help children live happier healthier lives.

Ways to Help Children Become Healthy

1. Accept the fact that you are a role model. Youth who observe your behavior use the information they receive from your behavior to answer questions about themselves and the world around them. What messages do you want recorded under your name?

2. Limit the amount of personal information you share with children. Make a personal commitment to not 'dump your trash' in their lives. Consider their needs when making decisions about bringing someone home to live their house.

3. Become more child -sensitive. Behave in a way that strengthens a child's sense of security, sense of belonging, sense of purpose, sense of competence and self-image. It is counterproductive to use blame, shame, guilt, self-righteousness as disciplinary tools. Denigrating children's natural characteristics e.g. calling them 'black, ugly, picky head, worthless hos' and faggots at every given opportunity undermines their self-esteem. Insulting a child's ethnicity, religion, neighborhood, socioeconomic status, parents or any factor that is outside of the child's control is cruel. Children do not choose their parents, where they live or their physical features etc.

4. Humanize your disciplinary tactics. Slapping a child in the face, kicking a child to the ground is dehumanizing behaviour.

5. Make every effort to not destroy children's trust and confidentiality. Gossiping about issues confided in you, throwing children's confidential histories back at them when you become angry are behaviors that undermine trust.

6. Take a stand against situations where you know children are being preyed upon. Expose predators or those seeking opportunities to take advantage of the naivety of youth. Worry less about how unpopular you will become if you expose wrong doing. Remember that no matter what children may have experienced, no matter how they protest structure and claim maturity, they are still not adults. They need your support. Beating them, and or cursing

them when they tell you that someone is hurting them will leave them open to more abuse.

7. Maintain high, realistic standards for behavior regardless of the situation the child is facing. Many youths are resilient. Make sure that you do not lower your standard of expected behavior if you (we ourselves) were not able to attain those standards in our own life (lives).

   In an ideal world, all adults would be perfect and not need to worry about charges of hypocrisy. However, we need to be bold about challenging our limits. Someone who became a parent at age fourteen may feel he/she has no moral right to expect children to delay parenting. Even with this handicap, advocate for and expect healthy moral, social, spiritual, emotional behavior from our children. We all have been wounded in some way but we all can contribute to the healing.

8. In trying to help, attack the problem and not the person, listen without interrupting, accusing, judging or jumping to conclusions. Dignify others. As far as is practical, allow for open expressions of thoughts and feelings. Resist retaliating with abuse when you hear what really is on a child's mind.

   If we can't be emotionally neutral in the face of outlandish comments from our children, then our children will tell us what they think we want to hear. Some adolescents will give us only the socially acceptable answers.

9. Gently guide and shape perceptions with a series of open ended questions that allow children to reason and work out solutions to difficult situations. Try to not preach or behave as if you are a perfect model. In the middle of a conflict, toss your points gently rather than flinging them wildly in an effort to stab the child.

10. Love, and do not expect to be loved back, give, and do not expect gratitude, or magical solutions. Do not offer help so that you can feel needed. You may not get what you need. It is the children's needs that are most important.

11. Remain humble and try not to believe that your influence is so awesome, that once you become involved in a child's life, the child's behaviour will automatically change. Children and adolescents have minds of their own and may not be impressed with your contribution to their lives if they are being helped by you.

12. Fight the cultural war in all aspects of our children's life. Choose not to let them wear what they want, drink when they want to, have sex when they feel like, smoke what they want, come home when they feel like, curse and fight with your support.

13. Get in your children's business. *Know and care about who their friends are, who they are chatting with on the Internet, which web sites they frequent, what kinds of video games they play, lyrics they listen to, where their gifts are coming from.* Monitor the behaviour of the adults that come in and out of your homes and your children's lives.

14. Behaviour change requires effort. Try not to present God as a magician that children can use to solve all problems without any lifestyle change on theirs or our behalf.

15. Be careful not to complain about how your life could be so much better without your children.

16. Spend quantity and quality time with your children. The Television, the Internet, the phone and the neighbors cannot replace good parenting.

17. Share the Blame. Remember, the clothes children wear, the lyrics they listen to and the lifestyles glorified in the media are all created and marketed by adults. Schools and homes are managed by adults. So changes in adult behavior will make a difference in the lives of children. In the mean time we do our best to train children and adolescents to minimize the damage they impose on their own lives.

18. It takes a village to raise a child but do not depend solely on the village to do our parenting for us.

Parenting Styles (Gwen Dewar, Ph.D.)

Authoritative parents are moderate in their approach to parenting. They set high standards but are warm, nurturing, and reasonable. They encourage their children to use their reasoning skills, and allow them to question parents' authority with respect. Authoritative parents emotionally support and motivate their children to become fully functioning, independent adults. Children derive significant benefits from being part of a stable family pattern where the parenting style is authoritative. Authoritative parents set limits, reason with their children, while responding constructively to their emotional needs.

Permissive parents are reluctant to impose rules and standards, preferring to let their kids regulate themselves.

Authoritarian parents demand a sort of blind obedience from their children and do not encourage the development of reasoning skills

Authoritative Parenting

Holds Children Accountable

Both, permissive parents, and authoritative parents are responsive, nurturing, and emotionally connected to their children. They both interact with their children. However, authoritative and permissive parents differ in how they manage infractions. Authoritative parents are highly responsive but still demand high standards of performance from their children. Authoritative parents hold their children accountable for their behaviour. Permissive parents tend to be negligent in this area, allowing children to do as they please.

Displays Warmth

Authoritarian parents and authoritative parents both support structure and rules. However, they have different ways of doing this. Unlike authoritarian parents, authoritative parents are warm and nurturing and they emphasize the reasons for rules. Children come to understand the consequences of appropriate and inappropriate behaviour. When children make mistakes, they appeal to their children's power of reason. Children are asked to explain their behaviour and to try and understand their parents' point of view. Children can debate issues with their parents, but they must respectfully do so. Authoritative parents are not likely to use shaming, or the withdrawal of love as techniques for managing their children's behaviour.

How to Identify an Authoritative Parent? Authoritative parents agree with statements like these:

- I take my children's wishes and feelings into consideration before I ask them to do something.
- I encourage my child to talk about his/her feelings.
- I try to help when my child is scared or upset.
- I provide my child with reasons for the expectations I have for her/ him.
- I respect my child's opinion and encourage him or her to express them...even if they are different from my own.

Authoritative parents are not likely to agree with statements like these:

- I let my child get away with leaving chores unfinished.
- I bribe my child to get him to comply with my wishes.
- I explode in anger toward my child.
- I punish my child by withdrawing affection.

The Impact of Authoritative Parenting on Children and Families

1. Explaining the reasons for rules has been linked with more advanced moral reasoning skills
2. Warm, interactive parenting promotes secure attachments and helps children become comfortable with expressing their feelings

and thoughts when in distress. These children are less likely to hold in negative emotions only to act them inappropriately at another time.

3. Parents who enforce limits help children develop respect for social norms and mores. These children are less likely to practice antisocial behavior.

4. Parents who avoid shaming and hurting children for academic mistakes may have children who are more resilient problem-solvers and better learners.

5. Encouraging independence can help to become more self-reliant, develop better problem- solving skills, and improve overall emotional health.

Don't Trust the Village!

When it comes to raising children, many persons are quick to say, 'It takes a village.' My mother never agreed with this sentiment. This was so half a century ago when the village was perhaps warmer than it is today. She did not trust some of the villagers. She had a rule, 'If my chirren do something wrong come and tell me'. Anybody in the village could bring us to her and lodge a complaint but only family members better yet, only her, had authority to hit.

This was so despite her growing up in an era where adults could beat children on the spot if they thought their behaviour was out of order. So, when folk in the neighborhood brought complaints to her attention and she did not whip out a belt and start beating immediately, some folk became angry. Because mother did not beat indiscriminately at the request of an offended village adult, some use to say that mother thought 'her children didn't come out a hole like everybody else'.

From way back then, my mother was afraid of some of the village psychotics. She was wary of giving any and everybody free reign to hit her children. She noted that she did not want to give opportunity to persons who were having a bad day to take out their frustrations on her children. When a neighbour brought a complaint, my mother would hold court and hear both sides of the story. What horror!

The enraged adult would claim that she was 'strengthening snake for frog' upholding a child's opinion against an adult. Parents were not supposed to strengthen their children in the front of grown folk. Children's opinions did not matter. What they wanted was an immediate beat-down. They called it 'satisfaction' They wanted mother to give them the satisfaction of seeing the child being beaten at their request.

Mother's first response would be to make the accused child apologize and do restoration when necessary. This just added fuel to the fire. Apologies not accepted. Only a beating would suffice. Many times the accused would believe they had escaped punishment only to find at 3:00am the morning, with no help around, and away from public glare, mother would light up the morning with her belt. This was a private family matter.

Other times, for capital offences, she would cut a switch (tiny sticks with leaves) and leave it standing by the outside door. Days would pass and just when the accused child thought the issue had faded away, mother would 'go commando' with her switch at the crack of dawn. Weeks could be spent waiting for the pre-dawn raid. Sometimes it came and sometimes it didn't.

The agony of the wait was the punishment. During the waiting period, there would be spontaneous lectures, teachings, scripture reading, sermons, guilt-induction, and verbal reprimands around the matter at hand. Opportunities would be given for the accused to explain their offending behavior. In hindsight, I think the waiting period was the chance for her to sense remorse and to decide if something more effective was needed to drive her lesson home. Yes, the village has its place, but it cannot replace effective parenting.

The Special Cries of Victims and Perpetrators of Youthful Violence
Throughout the years, I continued to be surprised by the ordinary, little boys that existed behind the records of violence. Yes, there were some offenders who were angry and bent on lashing out. There were boys whose ways of thinking were so skewed they rationalized their behaviour and remained proud of their record of violence. However, in a significant number of cases, boys had committed acts of violence because they thought of it as an act of learned socially approved behaviour.

This group of boys were not angry or cognitively impaired in any way except to believe that violence was an appropriate way to settle conflicts. Not only was it an acceptable way to solve conflicts, it was perceived as the approved way for real men to solve conflicts. This erroneous perception can exist in an otherwise nice young man who would sit and engage in positive conversation. These could be some of the "my good sons" for whom parents cry when they are arrested and go before the courts. As easily as this polite young man could engage in positive interactions, in an instant this mannerly boy when triggered could become inappropriately aggressive.

Boys functioning in a violent subculture have spoken about experiencing flash backs of past violent scenes. Some have spoken about being overwhelmed with thoughts of revenge. Some became depressed because of feelings of powerlessness. In response to these feelings, some increased drug use to ease the emotional discomfort. Some coped by isolating themselves further from their families and delving deeper into their friendship group.

Some boys were conflicted. They enjoyed the status of their gang membership. However, they were still sad about losing the respect of significant others who did not support their violent lifestyle. Others were experiencing guilt about their past behaviour. Some were still experiencing a general sense of loss, reminiscing over the violent death of someone known to them. Some had not properly grieved the loss of loved ones.

For those who had hurt opposing gang members, there were anxieties about possible retaliation.

The sexual and reproductive health of young Bahamian males is not a popular topic. Yet out of a group of 40 male students interviewed as part of an assessment project, more than thirty of them had practiced behaviours that made themselves vulnerable to contracting a sexually transmitted infection, STI. This same group risked becoming a parent. Teenage fathers are an underserved population. Several of the young men had girlfriends whose parents had insisted on abortions. These boys were going through a grief process with the support of their male peers.

All of them demonstrated a need for intense life skills training (systematic problem solving skills, skills for coping with peer pressure, communication skills, goal setting, values clarification exercises, responsible sexual and reproductive health and rights education including skills for avoiding unwanted pregnancy and STIs, drug use/abuse prevention training, conflict resolution, applying relevant Scriptural and secular principles to daily living, domestic violence prevention among many other topics. In addition to the need to provide information, there was also the need to correct misinformation.

Special Challenges of Incarcerated Children

Incarcerated children have higher rates of trauma exposure, posttraumatic stress, substance use and abuse, histories of sexual and physical abuse, issues of gender identity diffusion, learning disabilities and many other mental health challenges. There is therefore a need to understand the dynamics of the psychological and educational needs of such hurting children. A correct understanding of the dynamics would direct attention to the appropriate, evidence- based theories of psychoeducational intervention most likely to affect positive changes in learning and behavior (Benner, Nelson, Stage, Laederich and Ralston, 2010; Bryan 2012; Clair, Rossi, Martin, Cancilliere and Clarke, 2014; Conrad, Hasbro, Rizzo, Paella and Brown, 2014; Stimmel, Cruise, Ford, Weiss, 2014; Chassin, Manson, Nichler and Pandika, 2010; Crosby, Modrowski, Bennett, Chaplo, and Kerig, 2016 noted that there will be incarcerated children with significant mental health challenges that do not meet criteria for referral to a formal psychiatric service. It is important to understand how the children's histories impact their behaviour. The interview below sheds light on some of the misconceptions of working with incarcerated youth.

The Interview

Question: Why lock up children? Some children are locked up for criminal offences while others are locked up for status offences. What is the difference?

Answer: Criminals vs. Status Offenders

Criminal behavior is behavior that is illegal. In the formal sense of the word, delinquency usually refers to illegal offences committed by juveniles. A 21- year-old who steals is a criminal. A 14- year-old who steals is a delinquent. Delinquency suggests the commission of an offence that would be worthy of prison time if the offender were older. Male juvenile offenders tend to be detained for infractions that are clearly criminal in nature. These include theft, house breaking, stealing, receiving, drug offences, unlawfully carrying arms, causing harm etc.

On the other hand, around the world female juveniles tend to be incarcerated for offences that violate perceived standards of acceptable social behaviour for women. Associated infractions could involve running away from home or sometimes a pattern of expert use of obscenities, profanities, fighting, and an intractable absence of respect for authority. Such behaviours are referred to as status offences under which we get the rubric of 'uncontrollable'.

Persons tend to react with more emotional violence to an aggressive, sexually precocious girl than they do to an aggressive, sexually precocious boy. The female juvenile detainee is more than likely demonstrating behaviors outside of the parameters of acceptable feminine behavior. Conversely, there are not many parents anywhere in the world bringing their juvenile sons to be locked up because of an inappropriate relationship with a woman. If a young man developed a pattern of drinking, cursing or staying away from home, few parents would want to have them jailed. In many instances behaviours that are viewed as 'criminal' for a female juvenile are viewed as a rite of passage into adulthood for male juveniles.

<u>Question:</u> Do you think treating children nicely will change their behaviour? I think when locked-up children are misbehaving, they should be spoken to and treated in a manner that they understand and are used to. Soft treatment will not work for them.

Answer: It is assumed that children who are locked up are removed from a dysfunctional environment. The environment in which they are placed should be different from the environment they are coming from. The detention environment is supposed to allow them to feel protected and to assist them in developing their potential. The detention environment should not be as or more dysfunctional than the environment the child is coming from.

If the adults are unresponsive and their skills are incompatible with the demands of the job, then there is going to be a problem. If the parenting patterns in the Centres contain the same elements of infighting, cursing, rule infraction, poor supervision, denigration of self –esteem, emotional and physical abuse, as the environment that the child is coming from, then the child may as well be left at home. There will be little rehabilitation taking place in that detention environment.

Persons who "can't tolerate rude children" should never be hired to work in juvenile detention facilities. These Centres specialize in 'rude' children. Persons, who can only see the rudeness, show that they are unable to separate the children from their behaviour. Staff members are not expected to tolerate inappropriate behaviour, they are expected to understand the behaviour, analyze the factors triggering and sustaining the behaviour and respond consistently to reduce the frequency of occurrence.

There is a need to understand that old behaviours disappear slowly. They disappear as they are replaced with new behaviours in a secure environment designed to support change. Unassimilated detainees will bring to the table or use the behaviours that have worked for them in the past, i.e. manipulation, obscenities, profanities, deceit, defiance. These behaviors will be used at times to act out their feelings of anger about being detained for what they perceive as 'petty things' like sleeping out and cursing, violating parental authority. Some will use any combination of behaviours that will manipulate events in their favor. Persons who are intimidated or provoked by this natural display of survival or adaptive, should not work in juvenile detention centres.

Question: Should juvenile detention centres be operated by social service personnel? I think law enforcement officers, are better suited for the job.

Answer: Persons who make a comment like this are usually of the view that juvenile offenders are criminals and should be penalized as such. Persons who are unable to appreciate the humanity and youthfulness in offenders, should not work within juvenile detention facilities. This applies to both social service and law enforcement officers. Persons who cannot recognize the cry for help, who are unable to discern the strength, creativity and adaptive resilience hidden in the very act of defiance, will never be able to bring a delinquent youth juvenile into wholeness.

The canine mentality is needed. A dog can stick its nose into a putrid garbage can, rummage around and pull out a succulent piece of meat that no one thought was there. No one would want to eat a piece of meat from that bin. The dog however, is quite happy with its prized fine. Persons working with juvenile offenders need the ability to see the diamond in the rough. The nature of the work is such that there must be a willingness to cover the nose while cleaning the festering wound. The 'get well first and then I will help you' response does not work in such an environment.

Workers must be motivated to begin reaching out to the youth, and to begin working with them in the state that they are in when they walk through the door of the institution for the first time. As staff first give more and the offender accepts more, then more can be expected of them.

Question. What about beating? The Bible says that if you spare the rod, you spoil the child. It also says that foolishness is tied up in the heart of young people and only the rod of correction will remove it. So, we can only expect the offender to change, if we apply the rod of correction as the primary method of discipline.

Answer. While there may be a cultural support for corporal punishment, there are not many middle-aged, adult, buxom, plump, hypertensive Bahamian female or male officers, who can administer this form of punishment. It would be virtually impossible to outrun, catch, hold and beat a 15- year- old physically fit, trained street fighter who has the ability to drop a kick and somersault all in the same move. This is how they are likely to respond if they chose to not passively accept corporal punishment.

Strokes with a cane do nothing for someone who has survived being been beaten with wood, wire, pipe etc. There are those who appear immune to the impact of corporal punishment. For some corporal punishment is what they know. They provoke it, expect it, count on it, factor it into their decision making when deciding to commit an infraction. When reliance is placed on corporal punishment only, it's the offenders' game that is being played, on their home court, on their terms. Sometimes, the adults' most powerful tool is a display of respect for the offender. Respect is not what they expect as a first response. Respect comes easier when the offender is viewed as a young child, caught in a life that has gone amiss.

The Societal Conflict

The Bahamian community is conflicted about how to respond to juvenile offenders. If offenders are confined or given corporal punishment, there are parents, detainees, staff and community activists who cry 'inhumane'. If phone calls and visitation privileges are shortened, some parents, detainees, staff and community activists cry 'rights violation'. When detainees earn the right to go on outings and they go out well groomed, there are those who complain that the offenders' life seems to be too good, they are too well dressed, and appear happy. Offenders should not be happy, some would prefer that they live in chains, drag torn slippers and roast in the hot sun doing hard labor.

Adults who work with juvenile detainees should be encouraged to effectively use their training, wisdom, maturity, experience, patience, common sense, emotional fortitude, and spiritual stamina in the face of conflict. They can consistently refuse to be drawn into verbal tirades with angry detainees. There should be a marked and observable difference between the childish behaviour of the juvenile and the mature, adult behaviour of the officers. A frustrated juvenile detainee with a sense of 'nothing to lose' can verbally and physically digress into avenues that no right- thinking adult will want to follow.

In response, the impulse may be to want to 'slap the child's face in', but the laws of the Bahamas rightly limit the responses of officers in such provocative circumstances. The adult who retaliates with verbal and physical violence has lost the battle and comes under the control of the juvenile. Not only that, the adult has taught the child that violence is a legitimate response in the face of powerlessness and frustration. Adults who cannot model the kind of behaviors being expected of the detainees cannot function well in juvenile detention centres.

Corporal punishment sounds easy on the surface. Ethics is a challenge. Children say and do provocative things. One can never know when an officer may want to lash out because of shame, jealousy or other impure motives that have nothing to do with the detainees. Officers who lead double lives in small communities are vulnerable in detention settings. They should resist the urge to breathe an air of moral superiority on the same behaviours that they themselves are known by detainees to be guilty of in the community.

The duplicity will be made known and private affairs revealed at the earliest opportunity. Persons in known conflict- of- situations should make a special effort to stay away from work in juvenile detention settings. The power vested in their position will not help their credibility. The situation is even more challenging when and if the detainees are intelligent, stronger, more academically competent, street-wiser, more creative, arrogant, verbally competent, assertive and more talented than the officers. In today's world, juveniles with these characteristics should be expected and systematically planned for. Given these vulnerabilities in the environment, effort has to be put on educating the community to appreciate non-violent responses.

Shared Responsibility

Officers who work with juvenile offenders must realize, that peace only comes if the juvenile wants it. Restraint and detention are only possible if the juveniles decide that this too is what they want. Effective physical confrontations, in the face of a challenge by angry youthful detainees is virtually impossible. Officers may find that they are unprepared for what they have provoked. They may choose to confront but find that their colleagues may be too tired to back them up when they intentionally spark mayhem with inappropriate, provocative behaviour. The officer will be the victim.

Tired officers with second jobs who need to come to work to rest, should not work in a juvenile detention facility. In their fatigue, they irritate and inflame an already overworked team and fuel the advantage of disgruntled detainees. In general, effective back-up response may be an impossible feat if officers are inebriated, tired, mentally ill, locked on their cell phones, dressed in high heels, tight panty-hoses, tight fitted short skirts, or tight pants, accessorized with handicapping nail and hair extensions.

The attire and mental status of the officers can send a message of 'no intent to intervene.' It really makes no sense for an officer to be physically provocative towards incarcerated youth on the whole. It definitely makes less sense if the officer finds himself on a 'no intent to intervene' team. So, anybody who thinks they want to come to work in juvenile detentions so that they could beat and 'put a hurting on rude children', that person should reconsider.

<u>Question:</u> To what extent do we give consideration to factors other than sociology, psychology or criminology when dealing with offenders? The Bahamas is a Christian nation and I think we should be waging spiritual warfare against the spirit forces that are attacking our children and young people.
As can be found anywhere in the Caribbean, cultural neuroticism can still facilitate disorder. Persons working with juvenile defenders can expect to contend with an array of 'Anointers' who claim a direct connection to the Almighty. Ignoring the premise that God is not a God of disorder, these inspired helpers believe their Callings and private, Divinely Revealed Messages take precedence over science based secular theories or empirically- based best practices for therapeutic/rehabilitative intervention for helping offenders. At any given moment and without warning, some person, family member, officer can feel 'moved' and empowered to conduct a pseudo rite of exorcism with the laying on of hands, or deliver a private, divine directive or message from God. This form of 'divine' spontaneous inspiration is totally oblivious to the impact it may have on the child. Many times, the goal of instilling fear does not work, but what eventuates is a child overcome with anxiety who is more prone to acting out

Rehabilitation a Slow and Extremely Expensive Process

There is no magic solution for instant change. Detention or incarceration in and of itself has its own weaknesses and limits. A young person is detained to be removed from negative peer pressure or 'bad company'. They are removed and then locked down with 'bad to worse company', 24 hrs. a day. Sometimes there is even stronger negative peer pressure within the detention setting that prohibits change. Within the powerful social groupings that can develop in such settings, 'good' behaviour could be punished by the more powerful disordered youth, in a manner invisible to the most vigilant officers. Some youths may have to develop stronger deviant skills to survive within the setting. They may end up being more disordered than when they first came into the setting.

The following comments made by former detainees show that change if it comes, comes slowly.

'I no longer fight with weapons, but I still fight.

I still fight with weapons, though not as often.

I now only fight under provocation, before, I used to start the fights.

I still have a boyfriend, but I don't sleep out anymore and I am still in school.

I still curse and smoke, but I haven't had any more pregnancies.

I ran away from home, but I still go to school.

I still dress naked, tattoo my body, wear rings in my nose but I graduated from high school, the first one in my family to do so.

I still drive without a license, still sleep out, but I now get along with my family and I go to church.

Juveniles are Not the Only Ones to be Blamed

It is easy to blame the detained juveniles for the problems that arise in their lives. Clearly, there is need to evaluate the roles played by all stakeholders in this regard, caretakers, parents, predators, the community, policy makers, unions, media, juvenile court, probation officers, social workers, psychologists, administrators and staff at all levels. All share some responsibility for outcomes but only the juvenile is locked up. Is the society prepared to continue to spend millions of dollars every year to remove children from their homes? They remain incarcerated for months or years on end, locked them down with 'bad company' in an under-resourced environment. These juveniles risk the stigma and destabilization that comes from being labeled 'girl school girl/boys school boy' so that the youth could be taught a lesson?

Why not use the millions of dollars to strengthen human resources and programs that keep the youth within their home environment, programs that strengthen family ties, hunt down predators and expose poorly adjusted you to intensive, restorative day programs? Why not try all of these options before resorting to long term detention?

Do Not Give Up

Raise your eyes high, look carefully and you would see
the One who created the majestic heavenly bodies and families
He being dynamic in power knows them and us even by number,
calls each one by name, not one of them or us is missing.
The Creator of the far ends of the earth cannot grow weary.
There is no understanding His awesome, demonstrated power.
He is the one freely giving energy to the tired, faithful ones.
Those who are falling, he strengthens making full might abound.
Children without fail can become overwhelmed and weary.
Adolescents <u>will</u> without a doubt, can stumble, hurt and fall,
but those of us who understand and are connected to that
Power, can mount up with wings like eagles, we can empower
and teach our children to persevere, to run and not grow weary.
We can show them how to walk confidently, and not to faint.
Isaiah 40 adapted

Epilogue

The Boxing Match: Fighting for Balance Against Misplaced Values

Round 1

<u>Balance</u>, flashed her engagement ring.
Her paralyzed finger proudly out, as she sings.
Her hardworking, fisherman mopping his face,
proud as parental approvals flood the place.
He glad she accepted him, a good fight it took
He ain't good lookin, and not much on he book.

<u>Missplaced</u> with her phony smile, set in frost,
in da other corner, staring confused and lost.
Why they so happy about that cheap, ugly thing?
She couldn't be proud a that small ring!
I wonder how much dat little ting cost.
Sweetheart, run now, save ya self a divorce!
Matrimony before Mattress-mony, no chile,
what kind a naïve, stupid, people dat?
Pig- in- the-Bag, and a small ring what don't flash.
You'll praisin, dat lil ring, don't send me
no cheap, ordinary weddin invitation and ting.
With dat small ring, you could be sure
she and her children ga sleep on da floor.

Round 11

Balance duck dat blow, her weddin to discuss.
Something borrowed, old, blue, a must.
Gramma Bessie's heirloom dress,
three generations did brides impress.
Rare family jewel, dat ole dress, with
gorgeous, old-lace, beads and special, yes.

Balance worried about something new too.
New hairstyle, is what she would carefully do.
Some corn rows yes and dreadlocks, yup.
Old fashioned head wrap elegantly on da top.
Don't need a foreign shop to look fine and shine.
Dis fashion statement will be the real me all mine.

Round 111
<u>Missplaced</u> pumped her fists, put her hand to her ear!
Oh my God, what disaster Balance plannin here?
Gramma Bessie's dusty, old, yellowed dress?
This gal wan kill we all with shame and distress,
Lord have mercy, ole cloth tie around her dry head?
Slackness and Shameness, gal, will kill her dead.
She can't see how she shape bad and her back fat!
And she want tack Bessie gown stiffening on ta dat?
Girl them guest will dead with heart attack!

<u>Balance</u> moved to the side and dodged that low blow,
A thing old, new, now time for things borrowed and blue.
Borrow those precious, hand-made flowers from her class.
Those plain but precious flowers, year after year did last
should go well with family bridal party wearing blue,
made up of all her sisters and their playful children too.

October wedding would be perfect in my small church,
near my own beautiful flower garden by the old school.
Reception after, in Taxi Union Hall, an ole fashioned,
home- cooked- neighborhood ball for one and all.
Gift to register at Mr. Carey- everything -in- it -shop.
Less stress, more welcome for guest, at da One- Stop

Round 1V

Missplaced slapped herself, is this a kind of joke?
Balance six large sisters, who is cuss and smoke?
Bridesmaids, squeeze up in da small church yard?
Missplaced thought Balance head did finally gone bad!
But tell now, why they must wear outrageous blue?
Black people only look good in certain fabric and hue!

Blue in October, give me strength, I have to pray,
Sunburned plump people, in strange blue, what a day!
For October wedding dey all those who know, say, only
accessorized autumn shades, could come and play.
But it's her wedding, and she wants to lead da band,
as a cousin I need to help this ghetto girl out, man!
This crazy girl, ain't even realize, that the classiest,
the best of da best is what she'll be, if she leaves
this wedding planning to sophisticated, experienced, me.
Over the top and board, expensive, impressive
over budget, these the things most important ya see.
I into crafted and sculpted bodice and lace with firm lines,
symmetrically placed and diamonds, firm, tiny, tailored,
stitched with money without haste, covered with
threads of imported taste, I am Values Missplaced.

14 limos, flowers 12 ft. high, sixty doves loosed
to the sky, imported veil, layered to the hip,
only rare, unable to afford, imported wine guests sip.
No children in dis weddin to play, at home is where
dem ogly critters suppose to stay, hidden away.
And Balance before you think bout starting a riot,
listen, sit down and plan dem bridesmaids' diet.

Round V

<u>Balance</u>, weaving, bobbing, smiling with class,
telling Missplaced, her hand too fast and that
despite Missplaced absence her *real* friends were
coming, of that she was sure, so she's planning
on renting, a tent for space should they need more,
a tent, Balance did know, would be the final blow
to Missplaced sophisticated face, while droppin her jaw
and knocking her meddling snobbishness to the floor.

Missplaced lay knocked out, this count her last.
Smart girl this Balance, but she ain't had no class!
Where is this tasteless disaster of a wedding headin?
She for sure now was not gern ta dat jokey weddin!
No sir, she ain't comin out a her comfortable house.
She ga stick her head through her French winda
and watch how dat disorganized big circus turn out.

Round V1

Wedding Day: nuff chatter, Real Excitement mixin batter!
Curry soakin over meat, slow plantain, n' peas in dough.
Women compete for biggest sacrifice to marriage feast.
Jewels from secret places, barbers adding youth to old faces.
Pink Rollers, listenin under head tie, hear, Move, Spank!
Don't touch dat food and stay away from the drinks tank!

<u>Missplaced</u> watched the wedding circus, she in despair
Beauty really did tie that rag roun her unpermed hair!
Rented tables, and tent, home cook curry, behold this
ghetto gal Balance didn't een even look shame or worried!
She had da nerve to wear her old Gramma weddin sack!
Ole piece a rag for trail and veil running down her back!
Balance had to be so shame by now hearing that unholy crowd!

But see here, Style and Shape aint'gettin long, no sir.
Dem thick bridesmaids look hot up in dem blue ball gowns.
I know by now Balance want hide but stay, take the blame.
Then hide later in your tears on the honeymoon plane.

TKO

<u>Balance</u> ready, with time didn't flirt, fabric from Gramma wedding skirt, on gracefully locked hair was perched, sixty-year old cloth of faithfulness, weaving hair twice, tightly around, then falling, cascading proudly down, smiling in spell to the floor, with aged, intimate beads, sparkling, streaming, blessings aglow in the sunlight flowing past, beaming silent, pleased, yes patient onlookers, gasp, children bring her special flowers too, two hearts joined in ceremony of love, simple, true, blessed, balanced, authentic, new,

<u>Balance</u> and Wonderment moved happily in twos, slowly, through beautiful flowered aisles and smiling pews, in soft music, with her sisters' children in breathtaking hues, move with grace in a kaleidoscope of aquamarine blues. Dresses short, blue, floor length dresses, blue tailored suits and cute blue ball gowns and dresses, humbly graced hearts and souls of mesmerized town.

Cheers rupture the celebration, as Fisherman's extra uninvited, happy guests tumbled from ceremony to tent spread out in grand style in the transformed Union Hall parking lot, proud neighbourhood chefs uncovered their spicy and mild, specialty pots to start Ball of Fisherman-Balance, a well-chosen spot. Balance happy, unable to believe the order and grace, everything was smooth falling wonderfully, calmly in place, a left, and a right, this match was over she won for sure, Missplaced must be furious or passed out on her house floor. Common sense, faith, family values, confidence, humility win once more.

References

Benner G.J., J. Nelson, J.R., Stage, S.A., Laederich, M. & Ralston, N.C. (2010). Sex differences on MAYSI-2 mental health symptoms of juvenile detainees: Impact on status offenses and delinquency. *The Journal of Behavior Analysis of Offender and Victim Treatment and Prevention*, 2(1), 37-50.http://dx.doi.org/10.1037/h0100469

Bryan, A.D., (2012) Marijuana use and risky sexual behavior among high-risk adolescents: Trajectories, risk factors, and event-level relationships. *Developmental Psychology* 2012, 48, No.5, 1429 –1442 doi: 10.1037/a0027547 American Psychological Association

Chassin, L., Mansion, A.D., Nichter, B., Danielle Pandika, D., (2016) Substance use and substance use disorders as risk factors for juvenile offending. In APA *Handbook of Psychology and Juvenile Justice.* 277-305. http://psycnet.apa.org/books/14643/013.pdf

Conrad, S.M., Hasbro, B., and Christie J. R., Placella, N., Brown, L.K (2014). Gender differences in recidivism rates for juvenile justice youth: The Impact of sexual abuse. *Law and Human Behavior,* 38(4), 305–314.doi: 10.1037/lhb0000062 http://psycnet.apa.org/journals/lhb/38/4/305.pdf&uid=2013-35905-001&db=PA

Crosby, A., Modrowski, C. A, Bennett, C., Chaplo, S.D., and Kerig, P. (2016). Screening for PTSD among detained adolescents: Implications of the changesintheDSM–5.*PsychologicalTrauma:Theory,Research,Practice,and Policy* 8, (4), http://dx.doi.org/10.1037/tra000015 American Psychological Association

Kretschmar, J.M., Butcher, F., Kanary, P. J., and Devens, R., (2015) Responding to the mental health and substance abuse needs of youth in the juvenile justice system: Ohio's behavioral health/juvenile justice initiative. *American Journal of Orthopsychiatry.* Nov; 85(6), .515-21. doi: 10.1037/ort0000139. http://psycnet.apa.org/journals/ort/85/6/515.pdf

Stimmel, M.,A.; Cruise, K.R.; Ford, J. D.; Weiss, R A. (2014) Trauma exposure, posttraumatic stress disorder symptomatology, and aggression in male juvenile offenders. Psychological Trauma: Theory, Research, Practice, and Policy, 6(2), 184-19. doi: http://dx.doi.org/10.1037/a0032509

About the Author

Valerie is a Licensed Clinical Psychologist with the Health Professions Council of the Bahamas: Professional Specialty: Children and Adolescents. She has practiced as a Professional Child and Adolescent Specialist in Psychology and Education for over two decades after working for six years as a School Social Worker. She is a graduate of the traditional Government High School, Elmira College New York, the Postgraduate Clinical Psychology Program of Faculty of Medical Sciences University of the West Indies (Jamaica Campus) and the Department of Graduate Education at Northern Caribbean University, Mandeville Jamaica

A former School Social Worker in the School Welfare Section of the Ministry of Education in New Providence and the schools in North, Central, South Andros with the Berry Islands; Intern Psychologist at the University of the West Indies Department of Psychiatry Kingston Jamaica (Adults & Children), School Psychologist and Section Head of the Psychological Services Unit of the Ministry of Education's Special Services Division.

Former Local Psychometric and Psycho-educational Consultant for the Inter-American Development Bank's Hopedale Project for Children and Adolescents with learning and behavioral challenges including children with autism and other pervasive developmental disorders.

Former: Part-time lecturer in Abnormal and Social Psychology and Substance Abuse Prevention with the previous Benedictine University; Drug Rehabilitation Therapist and Clinical Director with the Bahamas Association for Social Health (BASH); Former Clinical Psychologist/Centre Manager at the Bahamas Family Planning Association's Health and Family Life Resource Centre and its 'Touch A Thousand' Program which was geared at heightening community awareness of the prevalence and impact of statutory rape; Former Psychologist at Willie Mae Pratt Centre for Girls and the Simpson Penn Centre for Boys.

Member of the American National Association of School Psychologists, American Psychologists Association, Past Council member and Past President of the Bahamas Psychologists Association, Member of Bahamas Family Planning Association.

Dedication

To those children and families who are sterling examples of resilience and courage.

To my friends, colleagues (social workers, teachers, psychologists, counselors, probation officers, preachers and their families) who daily work in the trenches, away from the lime lights, seeking to hold lives and families together, these are the real unsung heroes.

To my inner circle: Knijah Anubi Awanna, Emerald Farrington Hepburn, Dr. Suzette Lyn, and her family, Marcia Laramore and her family, Kenneth and Scott Hepburn and families, Nellie Rolle, (GG, Prince Edward Hepburn, Carrington and Mildred Clarke Hepburn, Geleta Clarke).

To my original publishers One Rib Publications: Nassau Bahamas

To the youthful team of the 2018 Citizen Security and Justice Programme in the Ministry of National Security Nassau Bahamas; a new generation of helping professionals committed to levelling the playing field and bringing relief to disadvantaged youth

Tonika Stubbs:	*:Project Implementation Executive*
Everette Sweeting	*: Procurement Officer*
Chet Pratt	*: Vocational Training Specialist*
Nadia Cash	*: Clinical Psychologist*
Clarence Albury	*: Communication Specialist*
Herbert Cash	*: Chartered Accountant*
Dorcas Cox	*: Project Manager*
Alex Veyrat-Ponent	*: IDB Consultant*
Nalini Shiwram	*: IDB Consultant*